Horse Tales

John Giovanni

John Giovanni

ISBN: 978-1-963502-46-6

Previous Novels

by John Giovanni

MAC-124 No Way to Die

Three Queens All In (Sequel to MAC-124)

Dedication

I want to dedicate this book to the extraordinary person who has been by my side for the past 51 years, my beloved wife, Susan. Throughout the countless retellings of my tales, she has patiently listened and provided unwavering support. Her presence and encouragement were instrumental during the four-year journey of assembling my cherished "Horse Tales."

Also to my daughter, Dr. Ann Giovanni , son Michael Giovanni, his wife and my daughter-in-law Pooja Giovanni and grandchildren Jordan Giovanni and Olivia Gia Giovanni.

Acknowledgment

I am deeply grateful to Donna Soper, who once again embraced the challenge of deciphering and typing my handwritten book. Her dedication and patience throughout this process are truly remarkable.

A special mention goes out to Amy White, whose invaluable assistance played a crucial role in turning my cherished "Horse Tales" into a tangible reality. Her unwavering support and guidance have been instrumental in bringing this project to fruition. I eagerly anticipate the continued support and guidance from her Marketing team.

Table Of Contents

Previous Novels ii

Dedication iii

Acknowledgment iv

About the Author 1

Preface 3

Tale 1: A Horse Named Sue 5

Tale 2: Not Exactly Right, My Biggest Loss Tale 7

Tale 3: Betting Over Your Head 9

Tale 4: Post Time Is 1 P.M. 12

Tale 5: Talk to The Winner 14

Tale 6: You Can't Win Every Race 16

Tale 7: John Who? 18

Tale 8: A Wave Is in The Eye of The Beholder Tale 20

Tale 9: Butch's Winning Blunder Tale 23

Tale 10: All That Glitters Is Not Gold 25

Tale 11: Who Are You? 27

Tale 12: There's No Such Thing as A Sure Thing 30

Tale 13: Unexpected Upset 32

Tale 14: Maybe It's Me 33

Tale 15: Can't Understand You 35

Tale 16: A Christmas Tale 37

Tale 17: This is No Convertible 40

Tale 18: A Message from Above 43

Tale 19: A True Saint's Tale 45

Tale 20: The Pick Six Double Fix 48

Horse Tales

Tale 21: A Fish Tale 50

Tale 22: The Winner's Circle 52

Tale 23: Don't Stoop Too Low 55

Tale 24: It Ain't Over Til It's Over 58

Tale 25: But What if You Have No Proof? 61

Tale 26: A Lost Voucher Tale 64

Tale 27: A Shorter $6,000 Tale 67

Tale 28: A Jerry Bailey Tale 69

Tale 29: A Missing Clerk's Tale 71

Tale 30: It's An Official Tale 74

Tale 31: Gambling Can Be An Addiction 76

Tale 32: A Parking Tale 80

Tale 33: A Winning But Losing Tale 82

Tale 34: A Half Million Tale 84

Tale 35: I'm On Your Side 86

Tale 36: A Two-Numbered Tale 90

Tale 37: An Annunciation Tale 92

Tale 38: A Bag Lady Tale 94

Tale 39: This isn't a Steeplechase Tale 96

Tale 40: A Hoof in the Mouth Tale 98

Tale 41: Another Sister's Tale 100

Tale 42:A Physician's Tie Tale 102

Tale 43:A Counterfeit Tale 104

Tale 44: An Unfriendly Friend Tale 106

Tale 45: Count Your Change Tale 108

Tale 46: A Voucher Mistake Tale 110

Tale 47: A White Rock Gary Tale 113

Tale 48: A Hundred Dollar Bill Tale 115

Tale 49: A Smoking Clerk Tale 117

Tale 50: It's Not A Better Than Later Tale 120

Tale 51: A Betting Trainer's Tale 122

Tale 52: A Wrong Race Betting Tale 124

Tale 53: A Real Rosy Tale 127

Tale 54: Famous People Tales 130

Take 55: A Wife's Betting Tale 132

Tale 56: A Profanity Tale 135

Tale 57: An Apologetic Triple Crown Tale 137

Tale 58: The End of the Tail Tale 139

PROLOGUE 144

About the Author

It's quite extraordinary how John's life was intricately connected to the world of horse racing. He was born in Amsterdam, New York. For the first 34 years of his married life, he resided in the small village Hagaman located in the town of Amsterdam. Growing up just a few miles away from Sanford Stud Farm, right on the outskirts of the city, it's safe to say that horse racing ran through his family's veins. His uncle Albert Giovanni was deeply involved in the equestrian world, spending countless years as an exercise rider at the Sanford Stud Farm.

His other uncle and godfather, Armand Giovanni, trained horses at Saratoga Harness Track before taking a position as their track electrician. After this, he moved on to become one of the regional directors of the Capitol District OTB (Off Track Betting).

John was a middle school social studies teacher for 23 years, and worked summers and some weekends as a mutuel clerk for NYRA (New York Racing Association). Upon moving on to administration in 1991, he worked weekends as a mutuel supervisor.

(Page intentionally left blank)

Preface

Let me start by saying that everything in this book is true to my recollection. I will attest that only the last names of my family members and the famous people I met will be used. The one exception is that of a good friend, John "Butch" Morrell, who permitted me to use his name in the one tale about him.

I want to pay tribute to the New York Racing Association, NYRA, who have successfully run Aqueduct, Belmont, and Saratoga thoroughbred race tracks since 1955. Have they made mistakes? Of course, but they have always been a class act. When mistakes were made, they always corrected them, making the racing experience better for their patrons. I enjoyed working for NYRA for twenty-seven years, from 1982 to 2008, and I continued to hold a valid license for their mutuels department.

Keeping this in mind, I want to start by mentioning the two biggest racing blunders I made.

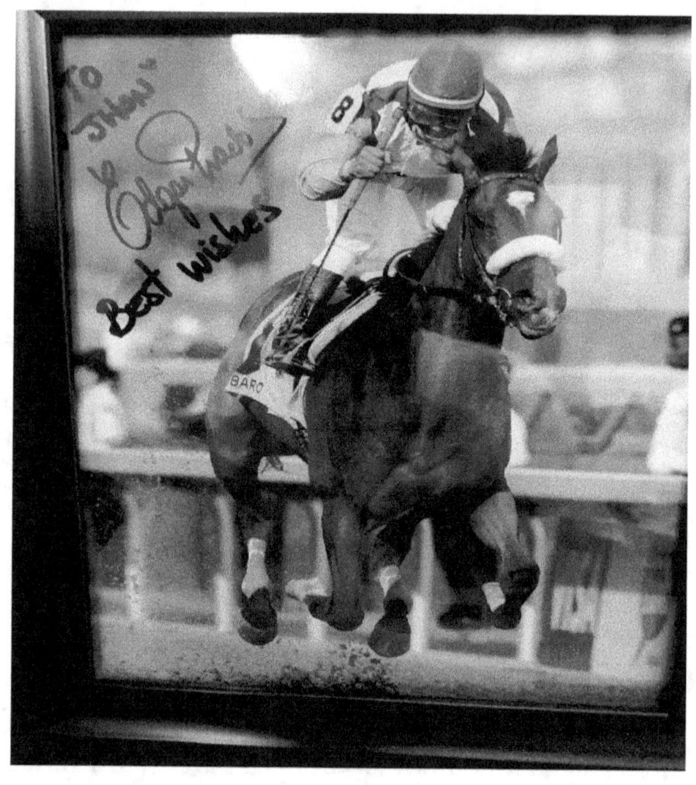

2006 Kentucky Derby winner Barbaro, ridden by Edgar Prado

Tale 1 -

A Horse Named Sue

Betting was frowned upon back in 1980, and still is today, for mutuel clerks and supervisors, but most of us enjoyed the experience. There was an old saying that if the employees of our department were not allowed to bet the daily handle, the revenue, would go down by ten percent. That's an overstatement, but there was a lot of money bet from inside the track years ago.

To give my readers a feel for this book, I would like to explain my two worst mistakes before regressing to my growing-up days at the tracks with my family. I worked at Window 920 in 1982 or 1983, when I picked a daily double bet based on superstition. This was one of the bets where you had to select both of the winners in the first two races.

Now, there are "doubles" in most races, at least at NYRA tracks. A horse named Sue was in the second race that day at Saratoga. I punched out a ticket with the two favorite horses in the first race with the Sue horse in the second race. Most gamblers would say this is the worst way to place a bet at a racetrack, but I did this. I still like to bet this way! As fate would have it, one of my two horses in the first race won, and now if the Sue horse won the second race, I had a winning daily double ticket.

Interestingly, the horse with the Sue name was a real long shot. I could not see the track from my vantage point, but we had televisions all around us. They displayed the potential odds of the horses and their potential payoffs. My horse would return close to $300.00 for a two-dollar double bet. I was full of hope as the race went off because the fever of possibly winning does this to you. My horse won the second race, and I was excited.

The race became official, and I quickly inserted the ticket into my machine before customers approached my window. To my surprise, my screen said, "Ticket, not a winner." This can occasionally happen, so I reinserted my ticket a second and third time, and each time it said the ticket was not a winner. I started to panic and talk out loud about something being wrong. The clerk beside me said, "What did you bet?" I said, "The winner of the first race with this Sue horse that just won." She leaned over and said, "That's what you think, you bet. The horse you bet was number 5, but the number 6 horse won the race." Sure enough, I had inadvertently punched the wrong number in my haste. My ticket read 2/5, but the winning combination was 2/6!

Tale 2 -

Not Exactly Right, My Biggest Loss Tale

My biggest mistake came in 1984, and I almost quit that day. I'm glad I didn't because I continued to work for twenty-six more years and loved every day of it. Most mistakes come at the last minute before the race goes off. With a minute to post time, when the race starts, a buzzer goes off, signaling a warning to be careful. An elderly man with a wide-brimmed hat approached my window and said, "I want a $92.00 exacta 8 with all and all with 8."

This meant he wanted the 8 horse to finish first or second, and he would be a winner. I looked up from my machine before I punched the ticket and said, "Sir, this is a very large amount of money you are betting." He told me to punch the tickets. So I did and said, "That will be $1,104.00." He replied, "Are you crazy? I don't want that ticket," and he walked away. I immediately stuck the ticket into my machine and hit cancel. Just then, the buzzing stopped, and the bell rang. I now was the owner of a $1,104.00 exacta box ticket. I yelled for the supervisor at the other end of the bay, and with that, the other clerk sitting on the right of me said, "I hope you have a winning ticket in front of you because you own it now."

The horse lost, and I now had to eat the ticket. At that point, the bay supervisor arrived, and I explained what had happened. He had me close my window, and within minutes, two plain clothes undercover cops were at my window. They asked for a description of the person who had made the bet, and they escorted me out into the grandstand seats to look for the bettor. As soon as I saw the man's hat, I knew it was him. The officers politely asked him if he had made this large bet.

He acknowledged that he was at my window but only wanted to spend a total of $92.00, so he walked away. With pressure from the officers, he gave them $92.00 for the amount he wanted to bet. My money draw box was shy of over $1,000, which was now my responsibility. I was ready to walk away and hire a lawyer, but the one supervisor from another bay really liked me and explained that the track would agree to deduct a little from my paycheck every week, even if it took a few years. He said if I enjoyed working there, it was a good compromise. I took the deal and slowly paid off NYRA. I guess I made the right decision because not only did I work for NYRA for twenty-six more years, I was promoted a few years later to a Mutuel Supervisor, where I spent the rest of my racing years.

Tale 3 -

Betting Over Your Head

My father loved the racetrack but knew gambling could quickly become an addiction. Thus, he had a few simple rules. Only take to the track what you can afford to spend. If you have a hundred dollars in your pocket, that's your limit for the day. If you come home without your hundred, look at it as a day of entertainment. Never think you have to return another day to get even. Even if you go the next day, go with a hundred dollars and let that be your limit. He also said any money you come home with is a plus! One dollar, two dollars, even a hundred or more, you were entertained and still have money in your pocket—case in point.

Back in the '80, the technology was much different. A mutuel clerk could only keep a certain amount of money in their drawer. They should shut their window down and count the money if they thought they were near that limit. Any amount over the specified limit had to be turned in to the mini-dealer. (It may have been $5,000 at the grandstand and $10,000 at the clubhouse windows). Some people got a little lazy and would wait until the end of the day and make only one return. The problem was that they needed sophisticated software to monitor each window by punching a button. It had to be a huge problem to raise a flag.

Today, their computers will show what each clerk is supposed to have in their money box. If it is over the allowed amount, it sets off a warning to call a supervisor and dispatch them immediately to the window in question.

On this day, the old software showed a large discrepancy at one window. Since it was near my location, they called me to investigate. I did, and after having the clerk in question shut down his window, I had him count his money slowly in front of me. To my surprise, his money box was almost empty.

Remember, he had yet to turn in any money that day. There was a possibility that maybe he had cashed a lot of large winning tickets and had very little money left to turn in. I've seen clerks get down to a couple of dollars at the end of the racing day.

This clerk told me his money box was "Short." I called the computer room upstairs and found that the guy was short, over $50,000. They sent me a computer printout of his day's transactions. It showed an alarming circumstance of events. It started when the clerk said he made a $100 bet in the first race and lost. Then he bet $200 on the second race, trying to get even. He lost again and doubled his next bet in the third race to $400.00. He continued to double his bets and lose for the remainder of the ten races.

Do the math! He bet and lost $51,200 without any money. He admitted to having a gambling problem. The track security was called and placed him under arrest. While escorting him out, one of his fellow clerks made a nice gesture. He asked if he had a wife or friend he could call for him. What he replied was what only a compulsive gambler would say. He told his fellow clerk that he could do him a big favor. That evening, he had a tip on a horse running at the Saratoga harness track. He asked if this guy could place a bet for him!

Today this wouldn't happen because as soon as a clerk's money box goes over the set limit, the computer sends out a warning, and a supervisor is dispatched to the problem area.

Usually it's just a matter of being too busy to stop and count their money. No real problem. Too late for this guy!

Tale 4 -

Post Time Is 1 P.M.

Growing up twenty-five miles from Saratoga Thoroughbred Race Track, a typical August outing was for my mother to pack a lunch box and head to the park area of the track. I had waited all year to eat and play the horses, even as a ten-year-old. On this day, my older sister, Patty, was doing her ordinary thirteen-year-old thing, standing in front of the mirror and making sure everything about herself was perfect. There were always a lot of young boys at the track with their parents, and she wanted to look her best. When my sister finally came out of the bathroom, my father was pacing back and forth with a look of disgust on his face. "Hurry up, Patty, we're going to miss the first race!" My father had read every inch of the Racing Form newspaper the night before. He had his daily double for the first and second races all picked out.

We arrived at the track at exactly 1 p.m., and the first race had just gone off.

Once inside, my father asked the first person he saw who had won the first race. He said the number 7 horse, and he paid a high price.

My father had a look of horror on his face. It was a facial expression you see a lot at the track. The 7 horse was his choice to win the first race. Now he really started to pace and talk to himself. He didn't say a word until the second race went off. He watched, and as the horses crossed the finish line, he turned to my mother and told her to pack it up because we were going home. Not understanding what happened, my mother asked why we weren't staying for the next seven races. My father said we were going home now. He made us pack up the food as he explained he had picked the daily double, but he did not get the bet in. Just for the heck of it, it was a monster of a payoff.

When I recently reminded my sister, she remembered that day very well. She said my father didn't raise his voice. He just repeated that we were going home now. That might have been the last time my mother and sister joined us at the track.

Now you know where I got my superstitions from!

Tale 5 -

Talk to The Winner

A few years later, my father and I were again at Saratoga for a day of racing. I was a few years older and enjoyed being part of the action. Again, my father reminded me that we had a budget. If all the money from hotdogs, soda, betting, etc., were gone, we were going home. He had bet the first race, and we were watching the horses in the paddock area with their trainers, jockeys, and grooms. He pointed out a particular young jockey and said his name was Angel Cordero. He explained that he was from Puerto Rico and one of the best jockeys on the riding circuit. My father said, "Look closely at what he does as he's getting up on his horse." I asked what the jockey was doing, and my father explained that he was talking to the horse in Spanish and petting his nose. This is how he calms his horses down before they go out on the track. It seems to work because he won many races that year and was the leading rider at Saratoga.

As my dad walked to the window to make his bet, I asked if he could put $2.00 to win on Cordero's horse for me. He did, and sure enough, the horse won the race. When the race became official, we looked at the giant billboard and saw it paid $10.00 to win. You get a surge of adrenaline rush when you realize you have picked a winner. I felt excitement for the first time as my father smiled and told me we were going home if our horse didn't win, leaving the track for the day because he had bet the rest of the day's budgeted money to win on this horse. I never asked how much he bet or won on that race but only remember him telling me he just had a hunch this horse was going to win!

Tale 6 -

You Can't Win Every Race

My father had a first cousin who owned a local tavern and was a heavy bettor. He worked tirelessly at his bar, treated his family well, and enjoyed gambling. On this day at Saratoga, we ran into this cousin after the second race. My father asked him how he was doing. "Felix, I'm up two grand." Remember, two thousand dollars in 1959 was a lot of money. It's still a hunk of change today, but it was a small fortune back then. My father wished him well, and we walked away.

Remember, gambling can be an addiction, and in this book, I mention people who were addicted to gambling. No names were mentioned!

It was just before post time for the 9th and final race of the day, and we again crossed paths with my father's cousin. "How you doing, Felix?" he asked. "I still have money in my pocket, so I guess I had a good day." Remember, this man was up two grand after the second race.

He very meekly replied to my father, "Can you lend me fifty? I'm all tapped out." This man was up a lot of money but had given it all back plus what he had when he left home. My father reached into his pocket and gave him the requested money. I was speechless. "He'll be at our door tomorrow with the fifty dollars," my father said, unconcerned. The next morning you guessed it, he was at our front door with the fifty dollars.

He had gone home that evening and worked at his bar until the wee hours of the morning. He said, "Thank you, cousin," and returned to the track. Gambling can be an addiction.

Tale 7 -

John Who?

On another occasion, I met a jockey who had the same name as me, John Giovanni. He was a jockey who typically raced at Rockingham or Suffolk Downs in New England but was at Saratoga to ride one of his mounts that his trainer had shipped to upstate New York to run for one day. Thus, the name "Shipper" was given to horses from other tracks that came to Saratoga to race. I really don't remember if his horse won the race, but as the jockeys walked through the crowd accompanied by the Pinkerton escort, my father said, "Hey, John, can you sign an autograph for my son? The two of you have the same name, John Giovanni." He stopped, smiled at me, and signed my program.

Fast forward maybe twenty-seven years, and I'm working as a mutuel clerk at Saratoga. All of a sudden, everyone in my bay was looking at me. They pointed to the loudspeaker on the wall and listened; I was startled. "What did I do wrong?" They're announcing to the whole track, "Will John Giovanni please report to the main track office immediately?" I closed my window, locked my money box, and headed to the main office on the upper floor. As I reached the stairs to exit the bay, my mutuel supervisor said, "Where are you going?" "They just announced my name over the loudspeaker; they want me to report to the main office now." "No, they don't want you. That announcement was for John Giovanni, a former jockey now retired and the President of the Jockey's Guild." The jockey who signed my program years before was now the spokesperson for the Jockey's Guild.

So much for having identical names; my father would have laughed like hell had he been alive! It wouldn't be the last time I got caught with egg on my face.

Tale 8 -

A Wave Is in The Eye of The Beholder Tale

Nelson Avenue is the street in Saratoga Springs, New York, that forms part of the boundary for the Saratoga Thoroughbred Racetrack and the Saratoga Harness Track. Just past the "flat track," as it was called, was the harness track, unlike the flat track where the thoroughbreds run for roughly six weeks in the summer. (The meet used to be only twenty-four days, but they have been slowly adding racing days as the years go by). The harness track is open most of the year for nighttime racing. Today there is a Racino (casino), which is a good draw for people who want to play slots or bet on horses. The horses at the harness track are called "standardbreds," and as the name indicates, were not the high-priced thoroughbreds that run at the thoroughbred track down the street during the summer.

Well, I had an uncle who was retired from the Amsterdam Post Office. He worked as a trainer for harness driver Bill Lamb. My Uncle Armand was also my Godfather and a very hard-working, honest man. On this day, my uncle told my father he thought that this horse, whose name I'd forgotten, was training very well and had a legitimate shot of winning the race he was entered in that evening. My father let me go with him to the track that night, and as a thirteen or fourteen-year-old boy, I was excited to join the action.

My uncle said that when the horses come out on the track, he would assess how he warmed up and his chances of winning. If he thought the horse was sharp, he would wave his hand in a circular motion above the horse's head like he was swatting a mosquito.

The horse warmed up, and the driver brought the horse back to my uncle for a last-minute equipment check. My father and I watched very closely as my uncle's hand made what appeared to be a circular motion over the horse's head. My father said, "Did you see that?" "Yes, I did; what did that mean?" "Uncle Armand gave me fourteen dollars and said if he did that with his hand to play his horse to win as a two-dollar exacta with the seven other horses in the race to run second. That means seven two-dollar bets or fourteen dollars." My father and I ran to the windows, and I watched him as he placed the exactas, once for my uncle and once for him.

Twenty-eight dollars total.

The race went off, and you know most of the story. Our horse won, and the exacta paid over two hundred dollars. My father and uncle now had over four hundred dollars in winning tickets, and I knew they will tip me at least twenty. Ten or fifteen minutes passed, and my father was waiting, money in hand, for my uncle to return from the barn. As he approached, he looked down like he had just lost his best friend. My father was all smiles as my uncle came to us and said, "I'm sorry, Felix." "Sorry for what, Armand? Our horse won, and the exacta paid a good price." "Yes, Felix, but I never waved my hand to signal you. I thought he warmed up poorly and wouldn't run a good race." "But you waved your arm above your head." "No, I felt the horse's head and adjusted his bridle. He felt very hot and looked uncomfortable."

My father discreetly handed him his winnings, and they laughed. As you will see in other tales, sometimes you get lucky.

Tale 9 -

Butch's Winning Blunder Tale

Lucky doesn't even come close to a mistake one of my good friends, John "Butch" Morrell, made. He permitted me to use his name in my book, so I did. On this particular afternoon, Butch was doing his usual stop at the Amsterdam, New York, OTB (Off Track Betting) Parlor. He was into exotic betting, which is not just picking one horse but two, three, or four horses in one race. These bets are tough to win because the odds are high, considering the small number of possible winning combinations with a large number of outcomes. He swears to me that he never checks his tickets after a race.

Once the race is official, he tears them up and throws them away. This day he bet a combination of triple boxes, the horses that had to finish first, second, and third in any order in the race. The race went off, and his tickets were thought to be losers. The results became official, and he glanced at his tickets for some unknown reason. To his surprise, he had inadvertently bet on the wrong track. He turned the television to the track on which he had his last bet and watched the race he now had triple tickets on. Not only did his mistake win, but all three horses he had bet on finished first, second and third and were long shots. His triple paid over $11,000. Not bad for a mistake!

Tale 10 -

All That Glitters Is Not Gold

This tale took place in the early 1980s when I was working as a mutuel clerk in the lower clubhouse at Saratoga. It faces the lower clubhouse dining area, which is on the finish line. I had the pleasure of having one of our state lawmakers bet at my window all day. He wasn't a heavy bettor, but he won no matter what he played!

All I could think of was, I hope this man keeps winning because I'm sure I'll get a massive tip at the end of the day. It almost seemed impossible, but this man collected on almost every race, exactas, triples, win bets, place bets and show bets. It was by far the best I have ever seen one person do in one day at the track. I've seen people win much more but never collect on so many individual bets. He was smiling, and his entourage of friends was making quite a scene. It was probably the best publicity he could get for the upcoming elections.

The last race ended, and I saw him smiling in the crowd. As soon as the race became official, I opened my window, not wanting to miss this legislator cash more tickets and give me a large tip. Sure enough, he hit the last race and told me, "I have never had a day like this at the track. I think you were my good luck charm." I expected the biggest tip I had ever received. Instead, as cordial as he was, this New York Legislator reached up to his lapel on his sport coat and unhooked an "I Love New York" pin. I thanked him, figuring this had to be a special pin he was wearing, probably eighteen-carat gold and worth a few hundred bucks.

The next day before leaving for the track, my father-in-law, Al Luciano, a retired gemologist and jewelry store owner, stopped at our house to "appraise" the pin for me. "What's it worth, Al?" He picked it up and examined it with a magnifying glass. He laughed and said, "Do you really want to know?" "Of course, I do. This was a gift from a prominent state legislator; what's it worth?" "Maybe ninety-nine cents." What I thought was my biggest tip ever turned out not even to be worth a buck!

Tale 11 -

Who Are You?

If you talk to hardcore gamblers, many will try to tell you the track is always out to screw them. They were especially weary of a mutuel clerk who might intentionally short-change them. If the truth be told, there were five dishonest bettors for every dishonest clerk. Case in point, from 1991 to 2009, I worked as a Mutuel Supervisor. Out of the classroom and into my district's administrative offices, I tendered my resignation with NYRA. At least, I tried to. My supervisor, a retired homicide detective from Brooklyn, New York, wanted to know why I was quitting. I told him that now that I was in education administration, I had to work summers and could no longer work weekdays at Saratoga. "No problem, John. I want to recommend to the powers that be that you be promoted to a Mutuel Supervisor." Since the weekends were the busiest days, I could work just weekends at Saratoga and four or five weekends in New York for their biggest race days. I'm telling this tale because you would think I had a bit more track savvy by now. I should have, but my actions didn't always prove that.

So, a man with a very recognizable yellow Hawaiian shirt asked the clerk at one end of my bay if he could speak with a supervisor.

The clerk yelled, "Supervisor!!!" and signaled me with his hand to come there. When I arrived, I peered through the betting window and asked the man with the wild-colored shirt how I could help him. "My winning ticket won't get accepted at any of the windows." I asked to see the ticket and checked it against the race results. His ticket was a $32 and change-winning ticket. Before I let him cash it, I should have called the computer room and had them run the ticket number to make sure it hadn't been cashed.

Typically, when a ticked is cashed, it gets branded, but sometimes the machine records the ticket but spits it out unbranded. What looks like a "live" ticket is already cashed but just not branded. The man told me that he didn't feel well and just wanted to cash his ticket and go home. Instead of taking a few minutes and making the call to the computer room to insure the ticket hadn't been cashed, I reached into my pocket and gave him $32 he claimed to be on the ticket. He said, "Thank you, keep the change." How nice of him. Now I did what I should have done in the first place. I called the computer room, thinking I would give them the serial number on the ticket, and they cleared the way for me to cash it and get my $32 back.

"Sorry, John, this ticket was already cashed fifteen minutes ago." I felt like a penny waiting for change. My next call was for Pinkerton support, and within a few minutes, two of the track-armed officers arrived. I unlocked the bay door, and the three of us entered the nearby crowd. Standing out like a sore thumb was this fairly tall man wearing a yellow Hawaiian shirt. "Sir, I believe you gave me this ticket and told me it wasn't cashed. I gave you $32 out of my pocket only to find out you lied. The ticket was already cashed. You owe me $32.00."

He replied, "Get away from me, buddy; I never saw you before. I don't know who the hell you are." He said if I didn't stop harassing him, he would file a complaint with the officers I was with and have me fired. He turned around with his head buried in his program, and I realized I had been conned and couldn't do a thing about it. Maybe I wouldn't be so gullible the next time.

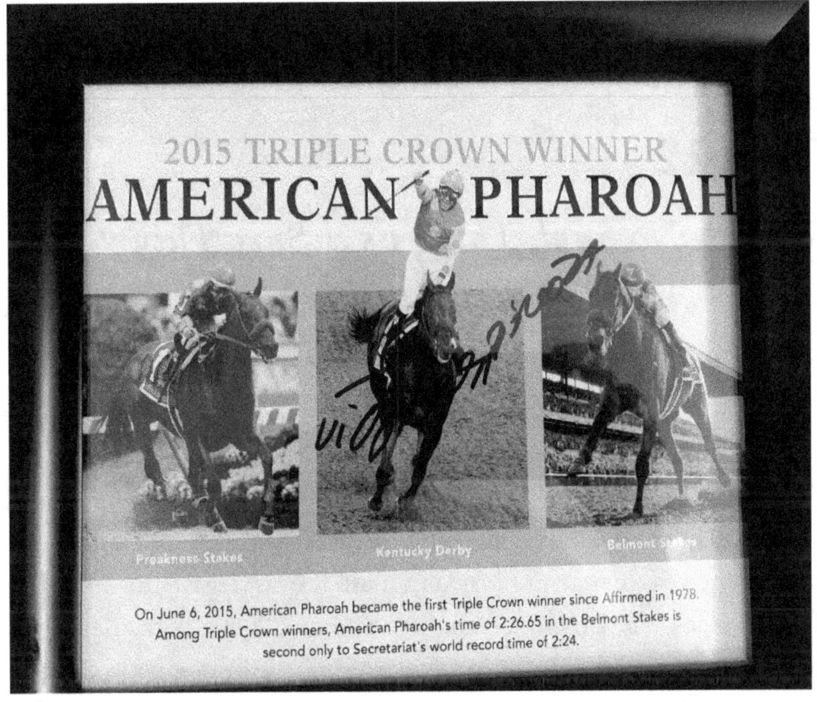

American Pharoah, 2015 Triple Crown winner ridden by Victor Espinoza.

Tale 12 -

There's No Such Thing as A Sure Thing

June 7, 2008.

Big Brown had won the first legs of the Triple Crown, the Kentucky Derby, and the Preakness Stakes. I flew up from my new residence in Florida to work the last leg of the 2008 Triple Crown races, the Belmont Stakes in Elmont, New York. Betting was now almost an unforgivable sin for NYRA employees, so I placed one wager that day, but I would use my OTB (Off Track Betting) phone account. A train went directly from Penn Central in New York City out to Long Island and made a stop at Belmont Racetrack. I made a conscious and what I thought was a very excellent decision to bet only one race that day, the featured Belmont Stakes. As I will explain in the other "tales," I have seen two Triple Crown horses run, but I have never been live at the track when they won.

My mind was made up before the train made it's scheduled stop inside Belmont Track. I would bet a sure thing! As I mentioned above a horse named Big Brown had won the first two legs of the Triple Crown and was the odds-on favorite to win this race and join some of the world's greatest thoroughbreds. The last horse to do this was Affirmed in 1978. It had been thirty years, and my gut told me he would win, but why bet him to win when I could make a safer bet by placing money on him to show or finish third? A horse of this caliber could do no worse than third place. In my infinite wisdom, I called OTB and placed a $50.00 show bet on Big Brown.

I felt he might pay around $2.40 for the third, and I would collect $60.00 for a profit of $10.00. I would get a hefty paycheck for working that day. I would see a horse win the Triple Crown, plus put an extra ten in my pocket. The rest of this tale is history. Big Brown ran last disappointing most of the crowd of over ninety-four thousand people. So much for a sure thing in racing.

Tale 13 -

Unexpected Upset

In August, 1973, The Whitney Handicap featured Secretariat, who had just won the Triple Crown a few weeks before. I was not employed by NYRA back in 1973. I had just married my wife, Susan, five months earlier. The couple who lived across the street from us at that time in Hagaman, New York, were Ann and Fred. Together with their friends, Judy and Henri, from Massachusetts, we went to the track that Saturday. Everyone was excited to see the Triple Crown winner, Secretariat, run that day. (He was the first Triple Crown winner since Citation won in 1948, twenty-five years before).

We bought seats in the grandstand near the finish line, and as the big race approached post time, I couldn't help stop myself from telling my wife and the other couples how great Secretariat was and how there was no way he was going to get beat that day. The other two couples and I all bet on him, but my wife insisted I put two dollars to win on a horse named Onion. Do I have to say anymore? Onion beat Secretariat that day in one of the racing's biggest upsets. I saw a Triple Crown winner run and lose. My wife has never let me forget it. (To Onion's credit, he set a track record a few weeks earlier at Saratoga).

Tale 14 -

Maybe It's Me

While on the topic of Triple Crown winners, I saw another horse who had won the spectacular Triple Crown of racing. I saw Affirmed race at Saratoga. Serious racing fans will remember that when American Pharaoh won the Crown in 2015, he was the first horse since Affirmed to accomplish that feat. That represents a thirty-seven-year lapse in horse racing history. On this August 22, 1978 day, Affirmed finished ahead of Alydar only to be disqualified because jockey Laffit Pincay had crossed in front of Alydar, forcing him to slow down. The racing stewards took Affirmed down and placed Alydar first.

In later years, I had the misfortune of seeing three horses who had won the first two legs of the Triple Crown, the Kentucky Derby, and the Preakness only to lose in the Belmont Stakes. I was working at Belmont Racetrack in 2003 when Funny Cide lost, in 2004 when Smarty Jones lost, in 2008, and as mentioned in a previous tale, when I made my fifty-dollar bet on Big Brown. I have seen three horses race live and lose the Triple Crown in the Belmont Stakes. I have also had the distinction of seeing two other Triple Crown winners, Secretariat and Affirmed, lose at Saratoga. Maybe it's me! As they say in Italian, I represent the Maledizione or curse.

Tale 15 -

Can't Understand You

While working as a Mutuel Supervisor, I always tried to give the track patrons the time and respect they might need to help solve their problems. On one of the hot Thursdays in August, the crowd was small, and so were the number of problems I had to deal with. As I walked behind the mutuel clerks, I saw and heard a furious elderly man yelling at this particular clerk.

The clerk shrugged his shoulders, saying, "I don't know what to do with this guy." "May I help you, sir? I'm the bay supervisor," I very politely asked the man. "I don't want this," he replied as he waived his ticket over his head. "That shouldn't be a problem, sir; this clerk will gladly cancel your ticket and issue you the one you prefer." At that point, the clerk interjected, "The ticket is from a previous race, and his horse lost." Seeing it was only a two-dollar ticket, I thought I would resolve the problem without much fanfare. "This ticket is a two-dollar win ticket on number two in the last race. Your horse didn't win the race, so you don't have a winning ticket; it has no value."

Now the screaming started. "I wanted Number 2 in the last race." "Yes, sir. You had Number 2 in the last race to win, and he lost." "I wanted 2," he screamed again. "That's what the clerk gave you. Did you want two dollars to make a two-dollar bet? Did you not want a two-dollar bet? Did you want the number 2 in an upcoming race?" I was running out of options, and this man was already out of patience. "What exactly did you want to bet, sir?" I asked him again... It felt like an Abbot and Costello routine at this point. "I wanted Number 2 to be Number 2." The light went on in my head. "Sir, did you want your horse, Number 2, to place or come in second?" "Yes, that's what I've been trying to tell you, idiots!"

"Not exactly, sir. You never mentioned you wanted the 2 horse to come in second.

Therefore, you lost, and this ticket has no value." I turned and started to walk away, and this man began to pound something against the clerk's window. He had a cane in his hand. He wanted to make a point. "Someday, you'll die," he said as he tried to poke me with the cane through the hole in the clerk's window. We both took a step back and looked at each other. We had a hard time not laughing. Then I blurted out, "I know I'm going to die someday, but I hope it's not today because of a cane cracking my skull." The patron walked away, a very unhappy camper, but in his haste to leave, he left his cane up against the lower part of the window. I quickly opened the back door of the bay and went around to the front of the window. I grabbed the cane and walked toward the man who was slowly departing. "Sir, I think you forgot something." He turned toward me, and I gingerly handed him his cane while taking a few steps backward. He realized he was wrong, but he wouldn't admit it. I guess we're all going to get old someday.

Tale 16 -

A Christmas Tale

My favorite spot to work at Saratoga was out in the park area. Beautiful trees, picnic tables, but most importantly, a few horses as they were let out of the barns into the walking area. The best horses and jockeys in the world would pass by before every race. I mentioned in a previous, "tale," I only had to supervise four mutuel clerks selling vouchers to bet off of and twenty-five to thirty SAM (Self-betting) machines to oversee.

On this last day of the Saratoga meet, always Labor Day, a lady approached me with a somber look. "Are you in charge," she politely asked. "Yes, I'm John Giovanni, the Mutuel Supervisor in the park area. Is there something I could help you with?" "Yes, you can." I misplaced or lost my winning ticket on the last race. I went to where I made a bet, and followed the path I took back to my lawn chair. I didn't find it."

This type of situation can be very easy or almost impossible, depending on a few things.

"Do you have any other tickets you bet on that race or a voucher from which you placed your bets?" She quietly reached into her purse and took out a losing ticket and voucher. I immediately went to the window of one of my voucher sellers and said, "Hand me the track phone." I called the computer room, and from her losing ticket and voucher, I asked for a computer printout of that machine's activity for the last ten minutes. More importantly, I asked if they had found a winning ticket and if it had been cashed. If so, the case closed, and the lady lost her money. She was lucky because the lost ticket was not cashed. I had them freeze the ticket so it couldn't be cashed. If someone did try, they would call me, and I would get the computer printout.

I could show that person the losing ticket, voucher, and the number on their ticket. I would assure the person that they did nothing wrong. It was an honest mistake. They found the ticket, but it didn't belong to them.

I returned to the park area where the lady was sitting and found her anxiously waiting for me. "Do you have my ticket?" "No, but I have good news for you. It hasn't been cashed, so I will record your name and address along with the ticket number and payout from my computer printout. NYRA will send you a check for your winning ticket in a few weeks. You could see the look of suspicion on her face, like, "Oh, yeah, they're going to send me a check in the mail." I saw her disappointment and said, "You will get a check in the mail; I promise you." She gave me the pertinent information and, with a half-smile, said thank you, turned and walked away. This was Labor Day in early September, and I had completely forgotten about it. Fast forward three months later, and I received a package in the mail.

My wife, Susan, said, "You received a package from a woman in Kingston, New York. Do you know who she is?" "No, I don't have the slightest idea, but I don't think it's a bomb. I'm going to open it." When I did, I was surprised to see a box of chocolates and a small note thanking me for helping her get her money, all forty-two dollars of it. I told my wife that this lady lost her ticket on Labor Day at the track. This probably cost her twenty- five to thirty dollars. It was one of the nicest Christmas gifts I have ever received from a stranger.

Tale 17 -

This is No Convertible

Working as a part-time Mutuel Supervisor meant working at different parts of the racetrack on different days. Sometimes I would have to leave my assigned area to chase down a lost ticket or go to another site to assist a supervisor in dealing with another problem.

On this day, I had to go to the upper clubhouse area, and as I did, I passed one of my track friends, who was a clubhouse entry attendant. As was this man, many of these men and women were exercise riders in the morning. It was the last week at Saratoga before NYRA moved back to Belmont Park for the fall meet. It was a custom to say goodbye to many of these people I had worked with and had become friends with.

As I walked by my friend, he grabbed my arm and said with an Irish accent, "Johnnie, I've been working this horse in the morning, and he's a monster. His name is Ragtop. I can't hold him back. I don't know if he'll draw in here at Saratoga, but I guarantee you the next time he races, he's going to win." I shook his hand and thanked him for the tip. I trusted this man even though sometimes you could receive a false alarm. They could wait until race day and give out the names of every horse in the race as a hot number. That is every horse except the one they thought would win. This will bring down the odds on all the horses in the race and push the odds on their horse up.

I looked at the entries daily for the rest of the Saratoga meet, and Ragtop didn't draw in. As the Athletic Director for our school district, the following Saturday, I had to travel forty miles to oversee our football team play a game in Troy, New York. As I had been doing every day for almost two weeks, I checked for the days' Belmont entries. Sure enough, he was running in one of the first two races that day, and the morning line on him was thirty-two to one. My wife was going to accompany me to the game. I informed her that we had to leave a few minutes early so we could stop at OTB (Off Track Betting). She asked why, and I told her this horse I had been talking about was racing today at odds of thirty-two to one, and I had to bet him.

We stopped, and I put ten dollars to win on his nose. My winning bet would return around three hundred and twenty dollars at his long odds. We arrived in Troy around one o'clock for the football game. Before we entered the field, we stayed in the car to listen to the live call of the race on the radio. He won the race easily, as the exercise rider had told me he would. I quickly turned the radio off, and my wife and I hustled inside to see the game.

After the game, which our high school won, we couldn't wait to get home and cash our winning ticket at OTB. Once there, I went to the nearest open window, excited to hear how much I had won. "Fifty-five dollars," the clerk said with a big smile. "No, I blurted out. That horse was thirty-two to one!"

"It might have been," the clerk replied, "but a lot of money must have been bet late on him to win. He went off at nine to two and paid eleven dollars to win. Here's your fifty-five dollars."

Remember the lesson, any winner you bet on is a winner no matter what it pays. I swallowed hard and couldn't wait to return to the car and give my wife the "good news."

Tale 18 -

A Message from Above

It seems like, over the years, history has repeated itself many times. Again, my late father's words of wisdom came back to haunt me. "Never bet over your head, set a limit, and don't expect to win." In the long run, the track never loses. Not when they take eighteen to twenty-two percent on average from the betting pools.

On this day, I was working one of the big racing days at Belmont Race Track. I don't honestly remember, but the chances are pretty good it was a Saturday. It was bustling; a few races had already taken place, and I had never had the opportunity to even look at the program. Thus, immediately after the first surge of bettors had collected their winning tickets, it got expectantly slow at the windows. I knew it was time to hit the men's room while I had a chance. I decided to add a few minutes to my break and walk to the next bay to change scenery. You had to walk up a flight of stairs and across the concrete crosswalks.

As I mentioned or will mention in a future tale, your position was such that you could see the racetrack or one of the betting areas on the lower level. Sometimes you could see both. These areas have big racing monitors, usually just above the betting windows. I stopped to look at the monitor, and I froze. The winning numbers on the board were 7/11. The 7 had won the race, and 11 had finished second. My dad had just spoken to me again. You see, he played the 711 number every day of his life on his way home from the post office. He would stop at the cigar-type store and bet his dollar with the bookie.

As I saw the winning payoff on the big screen, I heard my father say, "It wasn't meant to be." I turned to walk a few feet to the stairs going down to the next bay, when my curiosity got the best of me. I took my program out of my back pocket to see the names of the 7 and 11 horses. You can probably guess the name of the 7 horse: Felix. This is a very unusual name for a horse and one I have never seen again.

"What's the big deal?" you might say. So, my father played the number 711 every day of his adult life. So, the horse was named Felix. It was a total coincidence. Live and let live.

Forget the foolishness, but I couldn't forget because my father died on July 11th, or 711!

Tale 19 -

A True Saint's Tale

It was October 29, 2005, and the Breeder's Cup races were again held at Belmont Racetrack in Elmont, New York. It had been four years since the last Breeder's Cup races were held there. It was a much more relaxed scenario than in 2001, when the tragedy of 911 had only occurred a few weeks before.

Upon arriving at about ten in the morning from upstate New York, I was greeted by a friend of mine, one of the lead tote men. Totes were what we called the computer machines that printed the tickets. He quickly informed me to be very diligent because the track, on this day, was a fortress. He said he arrived about six a.m. and followed his daily routine of going up on the roof to check out the electrical system for the track computers.

To his astonishment, the roof was full of Swat Team officers already positioned around the entire area. They were facing the whole outside area of the track. Then he asked me to turn and look out the betting window into the crowd. What I saw was unbelievable. Groups of soldiers in fatigues armed with automatic weapons positioned around the track. Four years have passed since 9/11, but they were prepared for a worst-case scenario: a terror attack! Thank God it never happened on that day.

As was hoped for, the day went very smoothly. We were approaching the biggest race of the day, the four-million-dollar Breeder's Cup Classic. With about ten minutes to post time, a mutuel clerk at one of my windows waved his hand in the air to let me know he needed me, the bay supervisor. At the window, I encountered a beautiful well-dressed couple cashing some big winning tickets from the previous race.

I had to get involved because the couple was cashing close to seventy-five thousand dollars in winning tickets. Due to the USA PATRIOT ACT that was passed four years earlier after 9/11, a bay supervisor had to gather many personal identification items with tickets that large (I believe over ten thousand dollars) before the customer could get paid. I didn't know who this man or woman was and never saw them again. I believe they were owners or trainers. He acknowledged all of the legal paperwork and questions I had to ask with a big smile and then said, "You're going to have to do this at least once more." "Why?" I asked. "Because I'm betting fifty-seven thousand dollars on this race, and when St. Liam wins the classic, I will gladly do it again." He and the beautiful lady smiled at me and walked away.

It was now down to the last minute before post time, and the bells started to ring in the bay, warning the clerks that it was one minute to post time. Usually, this time before a big race, everyone hurried back to their seats or a nearby television to watch the race. Seeing no potential problems, I ran into the men's room, quickly entered one stall, and locked the door. I called NYS OTB and tried to place a twenty-dollar win bet on St. Liam, but it was too late. The betting windows had closed, and the horses were off and running. If you don't know what happened, St. Liam, ridden by Jerry Bailey, won the race and paid $6.80 to win. I would have collected $68.00 for my twenty-dollar bet. It wasn't in the cards for me that day.

I hustled back to the open windows and waited for this couple to return with their winning tickets worth around $194,000. As many bettors do, they returned to the window where they made their bets. I did all the paperwork for them again, and based on their $137,000 profit, they gave me a handsome tip which I immediately split with the clerk.Supervisors weren't to accept tips but...

Tale 20 -

The Pick Six Double Fix

On this day at Saratoga Race Course, the computers detected something peculiar with a winning Pick 6 ticket. I believe the first three races were run at another track in Maryland and the last three at Saratoga. Someone had picked just one horse to win in the first three races at the out-of-state track. Not unusual, but the bettor (s) had played every horse in the next three races at Saratoga so that they couldn't lose.

For example, you bet the 1, 2, and 3 horses to win the first three races, and they all won. The strange part is that the three winning numbers are combined with every horse in the next three races. For example, let's say there were ten horses in each of the following three races from Saratoga. The ticket would look like 1 with 2 with, 3 with all, with all, with all. A ticket like this would cost thousands of dollars even for a one-dollar bet, but because the Pick 6 pools are so big, the odds are excellent that a considerable profit still could be made. You have to understand that before the first race of the six was run, all betting on the day's Pick 6 was supposedly done.

What are the odds that someone had hacked into the computer and made a bet after the first three legs of the Pick 6 were over? They were guaranteed to win, but in the same way, the computer might get compromised; they are also programmed to pick these unusual bets. Upon investigating, they found one startling coincidence. The bets were made from outside one of the racetracks at one of the many OTB sites in the United States. The person or persons had found a way to bet after the first three races. Might it had been artificial intelligence?

The tickets were voided and were never able to be cashed. After the meet left Saratoga and went to New York, I never read or heard another word about it. But publicity is something racetracks don't need; in this case, I never read or heard to another word about it.

Wherever there is big money, there are always people trying to beat the system. Usually, they end up on the short end of the stick.

Tale 21 -
A Fish Tale

There are always people looking to steal from the racetrack. On this given day, a clerk shut her window and walked down the bay to where I stood. She showed me a hundred-dollar bill with an almost invisible pinhole in one corner; she handed it to me and said, "Look at this." My first response was to examine the bill and shrug my shoulders because it looked authentic. (As you will see in a later tale, I was not the best judge of real or counterfeit money).

"Feel the left-hand corner of the bill," she suggested. I did, and what I felt was a one-hundred-dollar bill with a very tiny pinhole. You have to know this woman was a veteran mutuel clerk who had been around the track for many years. "Do you know what this bill was used for previously?" she asked me. I said I didn't know, but asked her if someone could have tacked it up to a bulletin board or poked a small hole in the corner with a paper clip?

What she told me next was surreal. The hole in the bill came from a fish line that had been threaded through a tiny, almost invisible hole in one corner. She continued to explain that the trick was to walk up to a betting window and start to rattle off a series of bets as they placed a hundred-dollar bill in front of the clerk. Instantly, the clerk would see the bill in front of them and punch out the requested tickets for the customer.

With the clerk looking down at their keyboard, the customer would quickly pull on the fish line attached to inside their pocket. The customer had their bets planned to read a hundred dollars. When the clerk looks up and says, "A hundred dollars, sir," the customer sternly replies that he already took his bill as he started to bet. Nine out of ten times, an inexperienced clerk would think they took the bill first. In reality, many would apologize for their mistake!

Guess what? At the end of the day, the clerk is down a hundred dollars which they had to pay. The crook would then take the bill and use it without the fish line to make bets. What's that expression? The hand is quicker than the eye!

Tale 22 -

The Winner's Circle

My dream had always been to own a horse and win a race at Saratoga Racetrack. I thought standing in the winner's circle with the trainer, jockey, owner, and horse would be the thrill of a life time. I've never owned a thoroughbred, but I did make it into the Winner's Circle.

I had been invited on three occasions to join the then Mayor of Amsterdam, New York, Joseph Emanuele, in the Winner's Circle after the finish of the Grade II Amsterdam Stakes Race. In the two previous years, I had been too busy to leave my bay. You know what they say, "Third time's the charm."

Just a quick history on where all my love of thoroughbred horse racing came from. On the outskirts of the small City of Amsterdam, New York, in the Town of Amsterdam, sits the site of one of the most incredible horse farms ever. (Part of the track is still standing today).

Started by Steven Sanford, it was originally called Hurricana Stock Farm. Upon his death in 1913, his son John inherited the farm and won the Kentucky Derby in 1916 with a colt named George Smith. In 1927 he changed the name of the farm to Sanford Stud Farms.

The Sanford Stakes is still a race run at Saratoga every year in honor of this great horse racing family.

In the 1930s, one of my father's older brothers, Albert Giovanni, worked as a walker and exercise rider at the Sanford Farm. Consequently, our family always had a warm spot in our hearts for the traditions and history of the farm.

On the 30th day of July 2007, I was again invited by Joe Emanuele, Mayor of Amsterdam, to join him in the Winner's Circle after the finish of the Grade II, $150,000 Amsterdam Stakes. As I said, the third time was my charm. Again, I asked my boss, the head of the mutuels, if I could join the winner after the race. He permitted me as long as I had no pending problems. As fate would have it, the race went off, and I was free, so I quickly made my way out of my bay to the Winner's Circle. There I had my picture taken with the owners of Live Oaks Plantation, the winning horse, Most Distinguished, the trainer, Nick Zito, and the jockey, Rafael Bejarano, who signed the picture the next day for me; Mayor Joe Emanuele, his wife and their friends, Mr. and Mrs. Leggiero.

This was the thrill of my life, but there is one even more unbelievable thing about the picture. Other than the mayor and his wife, I didn't know what personal friends might be with them. As it turns out, the mayor's wife is a distant cousin of my wife, and Mr. Leggiero is a cousin of mine! It truly is a small world.

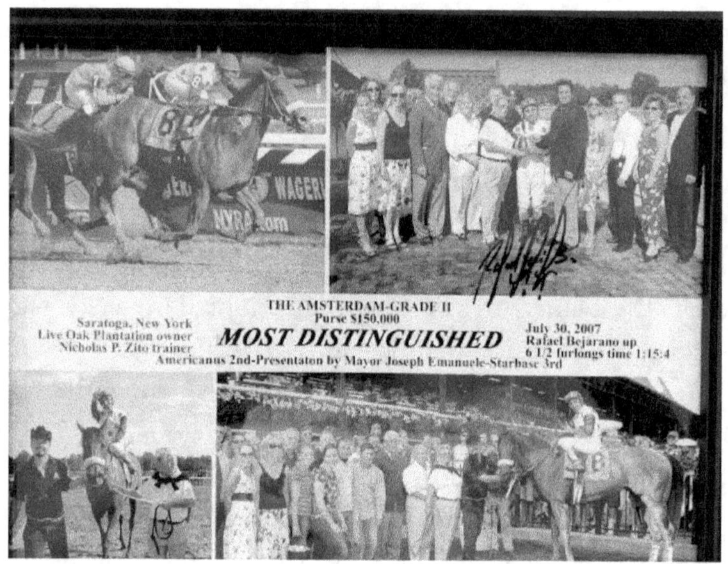

The Amsterdam Stakes Winners Circle

Tale 23 -

Don't Stoop Too Low

If someone were to ask you which type of people make the most money cashing tickets at a racetrack, who might you say? Surprisingly, I estimate that ninety percent of people who were posed this question would not answer correctly. Some would guess the horse owners, others the jockeys, agents, or trainers. Most would think that professional gamblers would be the answer. All wrong! (The best handicappers in the world still average around eleven percent in losses), the people who make the most money at the racetrack in the country are a group of individuals we call "stoopers".

They are not stupid stoopers because they have a basic tax fee unreportable and unedited income. So, who are these stoopers? They are the people who, all day but especially after the day's final race, walk in front of the mutuel clerk's windows, around trash cans, and everywhere bettors have thrown away or dropped what they think are losing tickets. They fill garbage bags multiple times during the day, as I mentioned earlier, especially at the end of the racing day.

On most racing days, the betting windows are open at 12 noon, and these collectors can be seen at self-service machines putting thousands of tickets in. Very few are winners, but they have so many to check that there are many winning tickets; they get vouchers from their winners and can go to almost any window at the track to cash them in. Some tickets are soiled by beer, food, or just plain foot traffic, which makes them unrecognizable by the self-service machines. It was not unusual for a stooper to be waiting at a window for it to open up. Thus, they would attempt to have the mutuel clerk try to cash the tickets that were not machine legible. If the clerk could read the serial number from the ticket, they could cash it by hand. On any given day, stoopers would cash hundreds of dollars' worth of winning tickets from previous racing days.

Combined with their vouchers from the self-service machines, it was not unusual for one person to cash tax-free five hundred to six hundred dollars worth of tickets.

There were two exceptions to this legal way of making a guaranteed profit at the track. If a ticket is paid over a certain amount (Six hundred or more dollars for a two-dollar bet), they will pay someone like their wife, girlfriend, parent, or friend with a low income to cash the ticket (s) in exchange for a monetary gift. This technically is illegal but very hard to prove. One famous jockey Hall of Famer's ex-wife made a living cashing tickets fifteen to twenty years ago. I don't know if she does this anymore, but it did happen.

As a Mutuel Supervisor, I would be called if payment of a winning ticket had been frozen. So, if the clerk had entered the code numbers in their machine, the screen would say, "Call the supervisor, ticket frozen, call a supervisor." The nearest supervisor would respond. I would intervene and ask the customer, usually a stooper, if the ticket belonged to them. Usually, they would look and say yes, but sometimes they would know it was an exercise in futility and walk away. If they did say yes, I would have to inform this person that the ticket had been reported as lost and payment had been frozen. I rarely got into an argument because they didn't want to be accused of stealing.

Well, unknown to most patrons at a racetrack, if they had bet multiple tickets and could produce one or more, we could trace the ticket in the computer system and find their winning lost ticket. For example, if the bettor said they had a ten-dollar win ticket on Number 3 in the 8th race the day before, you could trace the losing ticket number back to the winning ticket number to prove it belonged to them. It's a lot of paperwork, but if a ticket is reported lost, you can immediately do the paperwork with the help of the computer room staff and stop payment on the ticket. As long as this has been done, any lost winning tickets can't be cashed other than by the original person who proved their ownership. Of course, if someone had found the ticket and cashed it before the paperwork was done it was a moot issue. Their money was already paid out.

Tale 24 -

It Ain't Over Til It's Over

"It ain't over til it's over," or at least until the horses finish the race and it's been declared official. (Let's not mention disqualification). Another example of finding a lost ticket happened to me. I believed it was the Kentucky Derby simulcast from Belmont Park in Elmont, New York. The exact year I've forgotten, but the mistake I made I still remember vividly.

Since betting became frowned upon by all track employees, I would check in at the supervisor's room at around 10 a.m., do whatever paperwork had to be done, and head out to the station or bay. I had picked a few daily doubles and other bets out at home for the first and second races. I stopped at the self-service betting machine (called SAM) and bought a twenty-dollar voucher. I bet a few early daily doubles and a few quinella's. (Horses finish in the second race first or second, no matter the order), and still had a few dollars on my voucher. I punched finish, and my tickets and a voucher for my remaining balance came out. I put my tickets and voucher in the back of my wallet and proceeded to my bay to start work. It was unbelievable the minute they opened the windows for live betting. The crowd was immense on the first Saturday in May. Although the derby was being simulcast from Churchill Downs Racetrack in Louisville, Kentucky, Belmont had their live races to start the day.

Usually, once a race goes off, you can look at one of the televisions in the bay area (the station or set of windows you are assigned to supervise) and watch the race live. On this day, there was very little time to do this between races because of non-stop problems. It was wild from the minute they opened the windows to bet. The crowd was enormous, and on this type of day, it was deafening, and many mistakes were made by both the clerks and the patrons who were betting.

After each race became official, I would take my track program and circle the winning horses. I would put a big and bold 2nd, 3rd, and 4th on the horses that finished that way. I would then record the prices the horses paid next to their names for future inquiries. It wasn't until the bus ride home from the track on Long Island to Albany, New York, that I got to look at the day's results. As I mentioned before, it was a crazy busy day. I was so tired that I looked at the results of the first two races, the only ones I could bet. I had only bet sixteen and had a hefty paycheck coming for working. Not a bad day at the track! I took my losing tickets, tore them up, and threw them in the garbage pail on the bus. (Not my $4.00 voucher, which would be good for another day).

The next day I was relaxing at home and was just breezing through Saturday's program, looking at the results and pay outs I had entered there. All of a sudden, a light went off in my head. The results of the second race sent a jolt into my brain. I always automatically bet my wife's and children's ages in the second race, quinella. I'm a creature of habit, and my friends will tell you, superstitious when it comes to betting. One of my children's ages (Ann or Mike), I forgot which one, were the winning numbers in the second race quinella. I didn't waste any time calling the bus garage in Saratoga Springs and asking what they did with the garbage from the NYRA buses the day before. The lovely woman who answered said the buses had all been cleaned the night before, and the trash was placed in a dumpster! By the way, the value of my ticket was $125.00. What an idiot. I had thrown away a $125.00 ticket. But then again, I got over the brain fart I had the night before, and it wasn't over yet. I still had a $4.00 voucher in my wallet. Remember, I had $16.00 worth of bets off a $20.00 voucher.

What did Yogi say?

"It ain't over til it's over!" I waited until around ten a.m. when I knew the computer room would open for Sunday's racing. When I called, I explained that I needed a quick favor. With that, I gave the gentleman the serial number of my $4.00 voucher and asked him to check the tickets that generated my voucher on the computer.

Sure enough, the computer technician had my $16.00 bets, including one winning ticket worth $125.00. "I'm coming back down there in three weeks to work the Memorial Day Race; I need that serial number to cash that ticket for a person who lost his ticket."

I wasn't lying, I was that person, and that was my winning ticket. I had the voucher to show what bets had been made to substantiate my claim. He gave me the serial number from the winning ticket, and three weeks later, I went to one of the clerks selling vouchers at Belmont and said, "I have a number I would like you to punch in." He did, and sure enough, a $125.00 voucher popped up. I threw him $20.00 and said the patron wanted to thank us for helping him. That is the truth.

The bottom line, tickets in certain instances can be traced, and a patron's cash can be retrieved.

Tale 25 -

But What if You Have No Proof?

Jumping ahead to last November 19th, my wife, Susan, and I are sitting at the open-air Tommy Bahama bar and Restaurant in Coconut Point Mall when a man comes behind me to order a few drinks. When I turned around to say hello, I realized the man wore a Saratoga T-Shirt. Now, I have met so many people, not even from New York State, who love Saratoga Race Course, which happens to be the oldest major sporting venue of any kind in America. (It goes back to the Civil War in 1863). I asked this fellow if he went to Saratoga very often. He said he did, even though he was born in Buffalo, NY, but now lives in the Albany Capital District. Better than that, he worked as a mutuel clerk at the track.

I told him I was also a mutuel clerk from 1982 until 1991 and eventually became a Mutuel Supervisor until June 2008, when I worked the Belmont Stakes. We started to compare stories, and I thought I had a better one for everyone he had. This ceased when he told me what he had encountered working a few years ago at the Belmont Stakes. It was a horse tale I could not personally top.

The female clerk working next to him seemed to have a very nicely dressed, polite man come to her window for ten or eleven of the races that day. He was playing $8,000 to win on a horse in every race. She had carefully made a mental note each time on the number of the horse he bet. It would be too much money and a massive tip if he won. After each race, the man returned with a solemn look and would bet another $8,000 to win.

Obviously, he was wealthy but lost $8,000 a race and stayed calm.

The last race went off, and it became official. The lady next to him started to get super excited. This man, who had been betting a large sum of money on each race, finally won. She opened her computer and sure enough he had made a winning bet.

I told this man at the bar that the horse that won must have been a favorite. Betting that much on a longshot is absurd. Is it?

He replied with a big smile that the horse that won was 45 to 1. That equates to $92.00 for every two-dollar bet. So, do the math, 45 times $8,000 (plus your two dollars back on every bet) or 92 times $4,000. In simple words, his ticket was worth $368,000!!! Granted, he had bet $88,000 for the day, but his profit was $280,000, a little more than a quarter of a million dollars. Not bad for a day at the track. I would die to have a day like this.

So, why even tell this story? This clerk was waiting at her window for this man to return. Her tip would be enormous. People were passing her window, leaving the track, but she stayed at her window, just waiting for him to return and cash his winning ticket. As she waited, she saw this man pass outside her window. She started yelling, "Congratulations, congratulations, congratulations! You finally won."

He turned, walked back to her window, and politely said, "I didn't bet the winner in the last race." She informed him that he was the only person betting that exact amount of money on every race, and a winning bet was made on her machine. He told her he had bet a certain horse in the last race and lost.

"No, sir, you bet a different number, and it won. Do you have your ticket?"

He replied that he thought he had lost and threw his ticket away.

"Where did you throw it," she asked. "In one of these trash bins outside of this area."

The racing day was over, and as the news of what had happened spread, the clerk closed down her computer and ran outside the bay. Once the trash pails were empty, the ticket was gone. As you might have guessed, one of the clerks found the missing ticket before the maintenance men could take the trash out. That day, every clerk in the bay had gone to help and received a $100.00 tip. Around twenty clerks or $2,000.00. The clerk who had made the patron aware of his mistake received a $5,000.00 prize! She deserved every penny of it.

End of the story, right? Yes, but what would have happened if they didn't find the winning ticket? Besides the clerk realizing what had occurred, might the man have lost his $388,000? It all depends. The supervisor in charge of that betting area would file a written report with all the patron's pertinent information.

The clerk would have to substantiate that the betting information was correct and that the man had indeed bet $8,000.00 in all the day's races. Her computer log would show this. At the end of March of the following year, NYRA would cut the man a check for the winning amount. All would be well, but what if someone else had found that ticket? Could anyone, a stooper or another track patron, say it was theirs and cashed it? It was the clerk's word combined with the man who had made the winning bet against the person possessing the ticket. There would have been only a verbal trail. The patron would have lost. Possession is ninety percent of the law!

Tale 26 -

A Lost Voucher Tale

Speaking of a lost voucher or voucher left behind in a self-service machine, I was called to the upper clubhouse dining area at Saratoga. Someone had reported that a track patron had lost a large voucher. Upon arriving at the self-service machines there, I was greeted by the young man who was the SAM or self-service machine attendant who had reported the lost voucher. He said two men, and he pointed to the table where they were sitting, had put a $5,000.00 voucher in one of his machines, bet $800.00, and took their ticket. They were in such a hurry that they didn't even 'press finish' to get their $4,200.00 voucher.

(It must be mentioned that after a bet or series of bets are made there is a few-second lag which allows you to make more bets). If you don't press finish and wait a few seconds, your voucher automatically pops out. Many people grab the ticket they bet and turn and walk away. One of the two patrons had done just that. After getting back to their table and looking at their tickets, the one man realized he had never waited for his voucher,

They immediately returned to the SAM machine they had bet on and told the clerk they had forgotten their voucher. He checked their $800.00 bet ticket, showing what machine they bet on. The clerk gave me the information, and I used my walkie-talkie, yes, that's what it was, a walkie-talkie, to call the computer room and put a hold on anyone trying to cash that voucher. To my surprise, I was informed that the ticket had been cashed a few minutes earlier at a window downstairs in the lower clubhouse.

I passed on taking the elevator and quickly went downstairs to the window where the voucher had been cashed. I asked the clerk who cashed the voucher if he remembered the person's appearance. All he could remember was that he was a reasonably young college-age guy wearing a specific color shirt. When there are thirty to forty thousand people on a typical weekend at Saratoga, this was like looking for the proverbial "Needle in a haystack."

I returned to the Clubhouse dining area and explained this to the SAM Clerk who had called in the problem. As I explained to him that the missing voucher had been cashed downstairs and that there wasn't anything we could do to rectify the situation, he looked pretty stoic. I told him not to let it ruin his day.

Things like this are not uncommon at a racetrack, and it wasn't his fault. I then walked over to the table where the two men were sitting and explained that someone had found the missing voucher and cashed it. They were extremely cordial as they said it was their mistake and fully understood.

(It's nice having play money, isn't it?)

I returned to my bay area in the lower grandstand but decided after two or three races to go back to the upper clubhouse to see if the SAM clerk had seen anyone with that specific colored shirt pass by. Before he could answer me, the two gentlemen got up from their table and approached me. They were all smiles and laughing. All I could think of was that maybe they had made a few winning bets and recouped some of their lost money. To my surprise, they each held out their right hand and said, "Thank you for getting the money back."

They said the clerk had found their voucher, and they gave him a good tip. They offered me a bonus, but I told them supervisors shouldn't accept. I looked at the clerk; he was as white as a ghost. I knew he was guilty from the look on his face. Plus, the fact that the voucher had already been cashed a few hours ago meant it had to be a new voucher he gave the patrons. I stepped away and called the computer room. Might they have made a mistake? Maybe the original voucher hadn't been cashed? My suspicion was verified. The voucher had been cashed over an hour ago.

I approached the clerk, and he started to stutter. "Tell me the truth right now, or you will be in even bigger trouble." He then told me what happened. He had found the missing voucher sticking out of the machine and gave it to one of his buddies from Saratoga, who was at the track that day. His friend agreed to go and cash it for half, or $2,100.00. He said he was a college student and had never been in trouble. He panicked after I asked questions and had his friend buy a new voucher. I told him to pack his belongings and come to the mutuel office. I explained the situation to my boss, saying he seemed like a nice young man and a college student who had made a bad judgment. I suggested that we ream him out but dismiss him permanently. My boss agreed and took his mutuel clerk's license. He told him he could never work for NYRA again but was free to pay his way in as a patron.

I had the "honor" of escorting him out to the parking lot gate. With tears in his eyes, he again told me he had never been in trouble before and thanked me for my support. He knew he could have easily been arrested! I turned back to the track and never saw him again. By the way, I never mentioned he was tipped. It was his going away gift!

Tale 27 -

A Shorter $6,000 Tale

Yes, on this day, I again was asked via my walkie-talkie to go out into the picnic/park area to check on a problem at one of the self-service machines. Upon arrival, I approached the SAM clerk, and before she could say a word, this man ran over to us and started to scream that he had a huge voucher stuck in one of the machines. He said he only had seven minutes to post time and wanted to make a bet. I called the tote betting machine office, and they had a fellow nearby who arrived at our problem area in less than a minute. When he arrived, I explained to the tech that a large voucher was stuck in a machine.

The patron started to scream again, "I've got a $6,000.00 voucher stuck in that machine over there!" They ran to the machine, and the clerk and I quickly followed. Within seconds, the tech had the device open, and sure enough, there was a beer-stained damp $6,000.00 voucher stuck in the machine. He took the ticket over to the voucher seller (each self-service area had at least one) and read the number from the bottom of the ticket so it could be cashed. With the credit, he had a new dry ticket issued for the patron.

The TV's were now showing the horses were getting close to the starting gate, and the screamer grabbed the new voucher from the tech's hand, said a quick thank you, and ran to the nearest machine. I followed the man, not so much to see he didn't screw it up, but to see what he was in such a hurry to bet. He bet six grand on a horse to win in the soon-to-be-run race. With a ticket in hand, he had a big smile. He took a deep breath, said, "Thank you," and proceeded to the track to watch the race live.

So, what's the punch line? Had the horse won and paid a considerable price? No, the horse finished out of the money in fifth or sixth place. It's too bad we retrieved his voucher on time. He could have saved himself six grand!

Tale 28 -

A Jerry Bailey Tale

I believe what I believe, and whatever you believe in, a little, a lot, or not anything at all, is fine with me. I judge people on how they treat others, not their religious beliefs. I have many close friends who cover all bases, from very religious to atheists, with many in the middle.

One Sunday morning, I was running late to attend an early morning mass at St. Mary's Church in Amsterdam, New York. I decided to leave a little early and attend a service at St.Clements, a Catholic church close to the Saratoga Race Track. My oldest nephew, Ed Decker, and his beautiful wife, Dr. Christine Alexander Decker, were married there. I arrived just as the mass started, and in front of me was a man a little taller than me with a pretty woman and a young child. I don't know if the child was a male or female, but they seemed like a loving family.

For those of you who are of the Catholic faith, you know that near the last part of the mass, the priest says, "Peace be with you," and (before COVID-19) you would turn and shake hands with the people around you saying, "Peace be with you." This family in front of me turned with their hands out; sure enough, I knew him. He is a Racing Hall of Famer, now a racing commentator for one of the major networks, and one of the best, if not the best, jockey of all times, Jerry Bailey. He and his family could not have been friendlier. I smiled and thought, "He's not just one of the best; he and his family are wonderful people."

Tale 29 -

A Missing Clerk's Tale

It's a brisk Saturday morning in August and the last Saturday of that year's racing meet. The windows open up at noon for betting and cashing. Each bay has at least one cashier for IRS tickets which are winning tickets that pay over 600 to 1. Walking down behind the mutuel clerks, I arrived at the end window reserved for taxable ticket cashing. I saw a stack of neatly piled change and a lock on the clerk's money box. This meant the person assigned to this window had clocked in on their computer but wasn't there. The problem was that a line of angry people waited to cash the previous day's winning taxable tickets. I looked at the line of people and told them the clerk stationed at this window would be right back! Mistake!

At 12:15, with a growing number of angry patrons impatiently waiting in line, I got on the inside track phone land line and called the mutuel office. "This is John Giovanni, the supervisor in a bay station such and such, and I have an IRS clerk on window number ... checked in but not visible to the naked eye. They quickly checked their computers and told me the clerk's name.

At this point, the office was slightly upset, and they asked where she was. "She's not here, and I haven't seen her today," I suggested an announcement over the internal loudspeaker asking the missing clerk to report to her window as soon as possible. They did! Now I had to return to the line of people waiting to cash their tickets and inform them they had to go to another IRS window because the clerk was MIA. (I told a lie and said she was sick). The last thing I wanted was a riot outside my bay.

At approximately 12:45, this lady showed up at her window, but I looked at my watch before she could sit down and asked, "Where were you?" She said she was saying good-bye to her downstate New York friends in case she didn't see them before the meet at Saratoga ended.

Without a legitimate excuse for being away from her window for forty-five minutes, I had her perform the next set of required procedures. "Count all the money in your drawer, change included, open your computer and enter the amount of your return."

With tears in her eyes, she asked, "Am I going to be fired?" I explained that I didn't know what would happen but would escort her to the mutuel office upstairs. The woman in charge of the mutuel clerk's assignment asked her where she had been, and she repeated her good-bye story. She asked her to surrender her mutuel license and leave the track. She could only return as a paying patron. With her still wiping a few tears, I was asked to do something I only had to do three to four times in twenty-seven years. Walk the lady to the outside gate off the track. As we walked to the back parking lot gate, not saying a word, we reached our point of departure. I told her I was sorry this happened, but it's the racing association rules. Still crying, she turned and left, not saying a word. Little did I know I would see this lady again.

The Saratoga meet ended on Labor Day as it does every year, and a few weeks later, my wife Susan and I were in the Albany, New York airport, ready to take a much-needed vacation to the California wine country. As we were going through the TSA Security checkpoint, I looked up to my left and saw a familiar face out of the corner of my eye. In the next aisle, I saw the woman I had walked off the track a few weeks earlier. She was part of airport security. I tried not to look over my left shoulder, fearing that she would recognize me and seek revenge.

She never saw me, and we boarded our flight to the west coast. Had she seen me, I don't know what might have happened. Then again, maybe she did and decided to "Let sleeping dogs lie."

Tale 30 -

It's An *Official Tale*

On a very dark rainy afternoon in Saratoga, we had a tip on one of the first two races. I don't remember which one, but it was on a horse ridden by Marjorie Clayton, now deceased, but at the time, the wife of Hall of Fame jockey Angel Cordero. The track was soaking wet, and it was dark and foggy. The race went off, and we started to watch it on the television in our bay.

Almost every clerk in the bay, including their supervisor, me, had something bet to win on this horse. It could have been a dollar or a lot more, but it was supposed to be the tip of the day, if not the year.

We could hardly see the track on the television because of the terrible weather that day. As the horses came around the far turn into the home stretch, little could be seen, but the horse ridden by Marjorie went inside, outside, bouncing off horses on her right and the rail. The track announcer gave the name of the winning horse; sure enough, she had won the race.

Typically, all the clerks would be high-fiving and yelling, but there was a sullen look on their faces. She had bounced off at least three horses coming down the foggy stretch, and it could quickly become a jockey or steward's inquiry. Then again, when conditions like this exist, everyone seems to accept that contact between horses is not unusual. The race became official within a few minutes, and the payoffs or prices were posted. There were many quiet smiles as clerks put their winning tickets in their machines and cashed them. Seeing or not, seeing is believable.

Tale 31 -

Gambling Can Be An Addiction

While many individuals may enjoy horse racing and horse betting, it is essential to acknowledge that it can become a destructive addiction. Sadly, I have witnessed numerous cases of gambling addiction, and this story sheds light on one such individual's struggle with this addiction.

It was a hot, muggy day at Saratoga. People always said that if you didn't like the weather in upstate New York, wait a few minutes, and it would change. I'm in the picnic area where the horses enter the walking arena before each race when my walkie-talkie goes off. The call said a Mutuel Supervisor might be needed in the second bay of the lower grandstand. As I was stationed in the adjoining bay that day and at that time wasn't dealing with any problem, I approached the area. When I arrived, I found another supervisor beside a clerk who was counting the money in his drawer. This was not a good sign. The clerk had done something wrong and was being relieved of his duties. Rather than getting involved, I stopped and stood about ten feet from the interaction.

I listened as the supervisor instructed the clerk to punch out a receipt for the money he had just counted, shut his computer off, put the money in his bag, lock it, and come with him upstairs to the mutuel office.

As the clerk started to get up from his stool, the supervisor asked him to take the tickets out of his shirt pocket because they now belonged to the track. He refused, saying, "I paid for these tickets. The money in my bag is the amount on my computer printout ticket.

Besides that, a couple of them are uncashed winners."

I politely intervened and asked my colleague if the clerk's printed statement matched the money in his bag. He said it did, and I suggested that letting the clerk keep the tickets is best. He did, and they went to the mutuel office.

He was fired and told the usual story; he could return as a paying patron. I thought, "I'll never see this guy again." Little did I know that was not the way it would be.

A few weeks later, I had a patron outside my bay at an ATM. One of my clerks yelled that a man was having a problem with the machine.. ATMs were not part of the track's money system but were placed there by individual banks. It was always tough explaining to a customer that NYRA didn't have a thing to do with these machines. I would try to help by telling them to call the bank number on the machine because they were the only ones who could help them.

I went outside my bayside door where the ATM was located, and as I did, the man turned around and said, "Hello," like he knew me. He did! It was the clerk who had been fired a few weeks earlier. When I asked what the problem was, he told me his ATM card didn't work. He was trying to withdraw some cash. I was about to recite to him the track policy with these machines, which were a private entity, and that he should call the bank number on the machine.

Suddenly a light went off in my head, and something told me there was more to this than met the eye. I asked him if he minded if I looked at his card. He said no, but questioned why. I explained that sometimes you could run a piece of cloth, even plastic, over the strip on the back of the card, and it cleans it. If this is the case, the machine might take it.

He handed me the card, and I cleaned it with a tissue from my pocket, but as I did, I looked at it and saw why the card was not being accepted. "Sir, is this your card?" "No, " with a half smile on his face, he responded, "It's my wife's card." "Yes, I can see her picture on it." Rather than ask if he had permission to use it, I handed the card back to him and said I would turn around as he tried to reinsert it; I told him to enter the password as I was turned away. "I don't know its passcode," he replied. Case closed!

This man was a gambling addict who didn't have permission to use his wife's card. I just nodded and told him to have a nice day as I walked back to the rear door of the bay. I shook my head in disbelief as I unlocked the door and went inside. This might have seemed unusual, but ATMs and chronic gamblers seemed to find each other at race tracks. I have witnessed many problems like this.

There is one other such event that stands out in my mind. I was outside the bay I was working at because an irate customer complained he couldn't retrieve any cash from the ATM. Upon arriving, I asked if I could see his card and wipe it down. As I did, I observed it was his picture on the card, so I went through the whole drill again, turned around, reinserted the cart, et cetera. He did, and it still didn't work. Looking at the machine, I immediately saw the problem. "Sir, the machine says your account has a zero balance. Have you used this card today?" He said yes and told me he had started with a little over two thousand dollars. I asked if he thought he could have bet that much in the first five races. His head looked down at the ground and said he might have.

I told him I was sorry, but there wasn't anything I could do for him. I explained that if he thought there was an error in his account, he should call the number on the ATM. Horse racing is a sport that involves betting. The Sport of Kings, as it is often referred to, but as you can see, can become a royal addiction.

Tale 32 -

A Parking Tale

This is a tale of my stupidity, trying to get around the parking rules at Saratoga Thoroughbred Track. All NYRA track employees in supervisory full-time positions had parking passes allowing them to park near the track entrances. Part-time supervisors like myself had to park in the parking lots across the street from the track. It was a long walk away.

This was especially true on most summer August days when I had to park at the Oklahoma training track across the street from the main track entrance. I decided there had to be a better way, so I just drove up to the front entrance, and when the parking attendant put his hand up to stop me, I just flashed him my Mutuel Supervisor's badge, complete with name and picture. He gave me a quick look, smiled, and let me drive in. I parked, walked to the nearest gate, and showed my badge to the Pinkerton Track Officer. This was more like it, or at least I thought it was. I didn't realize that the man in charge of all the track parking was a few cars behind me in traffic. He never caught up to me, but he did see me park. I guess that's all he needed. Why? At the end of the day, when I walked out of the track, I couldn't find my car. My first thought was that I parked a couple of rows over, but at that time, the lot was almost empty, and my car wasn't in sight.

I stood in the parking lot like a "fish out of water," but no sign of my car. I saw a tow truck driving through the lot with his window down, and as he approached me, he stopped next to me and gave me the bad news. The head of track parking had given him my license plate number and demanded that my vehicle be towed off the track. He said getting my car back would have been a pretty hefty fine, but he knew I was a track employee, so he gave me a break. He told me to hop in and that he would drive me to my car. Once inside, I meekly asked how much the fine would be. He told me nothing this time, but I could not park in any reserved lots again without a track sticker on my bumper. He drove to a part of the track I had never seen before, the area beyond the backstretch where the horse walkers and people who did the most challenging jobs lived. They sat in front of their barn-like homes, cooking their supper over open wood fireplaces. It gave me a new perspective of where the actual track laborers lived during the meet. It reminded me of a scene from the 1930s movie, "Of Mice and Men," when America was in the heart of the Great Depression.

So, the bottom line was that I learned my lesson and would never park in a restricted-track parking area again. The only problem was that part-time employees like myself didn't get the bumper stickers. Being stubborn, I decided I should get a bumper sticker. I photographed a bumper sticker from a full-time employee's car. He was a friend of mine, but I can't seem to remember his name. I had an exact look-alike bumper sticker made and put it on my car. I was never questioned again! There's more than one way to skin a cat.

Tale 33 -

A Winning But Losing Tale

As a mutuel clerk selling tickets early in my career, we always looked for someone making large bets at the grandstand windows, not in the clubhouse where it was common. This was especially true when someone made a large Pick 5 or Pick 6 bet. (This is where you had to pick five or six race winners in a row). It was another rainy day at Saratoga, and a small crowd was betting even slower. This was both good and bad. It was good because back in the 80s, no one stopped the mutuel clerks from betting. I think it was allowed. They always said the track handle would decrease by ten percent if the clerks didn't bet!

It was getting near post time when a man came up to a nearby window and bet $4,800.00 worth of Pick 6 tickets. As I mentioned, this was not unusual, but this man was in the grandstand, not the clubhouse. This was the first red flag, the second being how the bet was made. He bet multiple horses in five out of six races, except that he bet only one horse on every ticket in one race. That horse was a filly in a maiden race. (A filly is a young female horse, usually four years old or younger). A maiden is a horse who has never won a race. That tends to insinuate that that horse is a great bet and maybe a tip from the unknown.

As word spread down the line of mutuel clerks, we all had bet something to win on this horse. It won the race but didn't pay a lot. Maybe six or seven dollars for a two-dollar bet, but we all made a little money on it.

After the sixth and last race on his ticket, this guy returned to the same window where he had bet, to cash his winning ticket. The ticket paid $4,200, which equates to a $600.00 loss on his original bet. To add insult to injury, not only did he lose money, but because it paid over six hundred to one, he had to fill out papers to file with the IRS.

The track rule was that you should bet a little to win a lot, not a lot to win a little. "Does anymore need to be said?"

Tale 34 -

A Half Million Tale

When there aren't enough winning tickets paid out on a Pick 6 ticket, that money goes into the next day's collection, so they can advertise that the money carried over from the previous day will be automatically paid out.

It was a sunny Saturday afternoon, and a guaranteed half million Pick 6 would be paid out that day. Say that no one picked all four, five, or six winners; every one with three winners would split the money in the pool. Sometimes there would only be one winner, and if the horses were mostly favorites, there could be numerous winners.

Well, you guessed it! All six winning horses that day in races five to ten were favorites. As soon as the race became official, a group of young men outside the bay I was working at that day started to scream and yell. They had a winning ticket with a guaranteed payout of at least $500,000. They had all or part of that money. With beer in their hands, one guy in the group ran up to a window with his buddies crowded around him. He handed the clerk the winning ticket, and when he ran it through the machine, the cheering turned to boo and angry remarks. (I won't mention their vocabulary). I saw there was going to be a problem, so I approached the window from behind the clerk and asked what the problem was. Screams of, "Where's our half million?" resonated through the metal grated window. Those eight men had one of the winning tickets, each paying under $450.00. Split eight ways, these guys would get around fifty dollars each, and it was my job to explain why their pool shares were so small. Finally, after much arguing, one of the guys called for calmness among his friends. Maybe he was an attorney, I don't know, but he took charge.

"We want proof of how many winning tickets were sold for this Pick 6." "No problem," I said. "I'll call upstairs to the computer room and get a computer printout of what you're requesting," I asked for ten to fifteen minutes to retrieve the information. The leader nodded his head, and they waited quietly.

When I returned, I had the printout; it showed exactly what I had told them. There were hundreds of winning tickets, thus the tiny payout. The spokesperson asked for a copy of the printout sheet, and I had to explain that many of the winning ticket numbers on that sheet had not been cashed yet. Thus, that information was private. I circled their ticket number on the printout, showing them how much they would get paid. It ended well, with the group disappointed but accepting the facts.

Tale 35 -
I'm On Your Side

I worked as a mutuel clerk for NYRA for my first nine years. Almost every day, I was at a different window, sometimes in the same bay, and on this day, I was working in Bay 1 under a great supervisor, whom I'll call by his first name, Al.

I was appointed to my first administrative position in the Greater Amsterdam School District in 1991. This created a work conflict because I was now required to work summers.

I called New York's Belmont Track and asked if Mutuel Supervisor Al could take a call from me. As always, he answered the call with much enthusiasm. Before I could speak, he said, "I'll see you next week when Saratoga opens."

I told him I had a problem. "What's wrong? Are you sick? Is someone in your family sick?" I explained that everything was fine, but I couldn't work anymore for NYRA because I had to work as an administrator during the week. He told me it wasn't a problem because they needed help on the weekends when the crowds were between forty to fifty thousand people. He said he knew I was looking for an administrative school position and anticipated that I couldn't work weekdays. He asked his boss if I could work just weekends as a Mutuel Supervisor, and they said they were happy to have me.

What I didn't know about this sixty-some-odd-year-old man, my mentor for nine years at the track, was what he had done in his previous life. Jump ahead to the first weekend of the racing season, and Al had me working with him for my first two days as a Mutuel Supervisor. Of course, everything went smoothly for six or seven races, and it felt like an easy transition. This was that way until a very irate customer approached the window in front of me and started to yell profanities at the clerk working the betting machine. "This asshole just gave me the wrong numbers! I wanted a twenty-dollar exacta box on these numbers. He punched out something else." "Well, sir, I'm sorry, but the race is over, and the computer can't make a change. If you had stayed in front of the window and checked your ticket, you would have seen the error. The clerk could have canceled your ticket and issued you one with the correct numbers."

This didn't satisfy him, and he began to shout profanities at us. He threatened to climb over the top of the bay and kill us. He apparently had too much to drink and wouldn't accept my answer. Suddenly I felt a large hand gently push on my right shoulder as Al approached me and asked the patron if he could help. The bettor told him the story, saying he would find a way inside and do us bodily harm. For the first of many times, I heard Al's calming voice as he said, "I'm on your side, sir," he kept repeating it as the man continued his tirade. When the man repeated that he wanted to hurt us, Al said, "You don't have to do that, I'm coming out that door to your left, and we will settle this."

Now Al was around 6' 2" and well built, but how would he calm this guy, probably thirty years younger, without getting into a fight? This guy was reasonably big himself, and being angry and intoxicated, it had the makings of an ugly scene.

My eyes widened as Al exited the bay door and confronted the man. He calmed him down immediately by having two fully armed track Pinkertons on either side of him. In a very soft but stern voice, he told the man he had two choices: he could start a fight and immediately be placed under arrest or quietly let these two officers escort him off the track. He then could return on another day, more civil and sober. He accepted the latter and was escorted off the track.

Al came back into the bay with a big smile on his face. The first thing I asked him was why this didn't scare him. His answer still resonates with me today. "John, do you know what I did in the first part of my life?" "No, Al." "I was a homicide detective in Brooklyn, New York. This guy was a piece of cake compared to what I used to do for a living."

What I didn't know but grew to know was, "Sir, I'm on your side" was his favorite expression. I flew to New York from Florida in 2008 to work the Belmont Stakes; that was the last time I had physical contact with him. He was well into his 80s and still working.

End of the story (tale), right? Now, the unique part is that you can run but can't hide. My wife, Susan, and I moved from Cape Coral, Florida, to Bonita Springs, Florida, in 2013, and we found the Bonita, North Naples area, to be a hotbed for great food. There was and still is an excellent steakhouse on Route 41 in North Naples called Flemmings. Our first time visiting the restaurant, I was looking at the menu and happened to see the name of one of the manager owners. He had the same first and last name as my track mentor. Just for the heck of it, I asked the bartender if this manager was working. He said he wasn't, but why did I ask? I told him I had worked with a man by the same name at the NYRA racetracks in New York. This remarkable man was my mentor, but before that, he had been a homicide detective in Brooklyn, New York. The bartender said that it sounded like the owner's father.

I left the bartender my name, and the next time we were at his restaurant, the manager was told I was the fellow that worked with his father at the track. He talked to his father and told him I was a friend. He took my phone number, and sure enough, Al Senior called. We talked for a very long time about our twenty-seven years of working together. It's a small world. (Al Senior has since passed well into his 90s, and my condolences go out to his son and family).

Tale 36 -

A Two-Numbered Tale

As a Mutuel Supervisor, we would arrive two and a half hours before the first race started and check our lists for signs of money laundering or other illegal activity from the previous race day.

Just before the noon opening of betting windows, many clerks would file in from a door that took them into the lower clubhouse bay. Some of the full-time clerks were also former jockeys. Some still worked as exercise riders in the morning before they came to work the windows.

There wasn't a day that went by where at least one of these former jockeys would walk past our open office door and say two numbers. For example, 3/4 or 7/6. What did they mean? It's simple. 3/4 means the third race, 4 horse. 7/6 means the seventh race, 6 horse. If the truth is told, the horses mentioned were considered "live." The horse trainer may advise the exercise riders not to work their horse out very fast. This was so that the clockers who recorded these times wouldn't know the horse's shape. They would get paid to sell their information to newspapers or private pick sheet operators. Then again, they might try to sneak in a good workout early in the morning before the clockers arrived. All very legal activities.

Percentages were good that the horses given to us would run a good race but wouldn't necessarily win. Maybe they were up against much better horses, and a third or fourth finish in a stakes race would be a good sign for the future.

Tips are tips and not anything else. They usually don't win! That's not to mean some don't win, but they are few and far between.

Tale 37 -

An Annunciation Tale

I was working in the old paddock area of Saratoga, which had been converted into a betting area many years ago. If you entered the track next to the clubhouse gate, it was a dark green building with a Pinkerton (track police) or two standing next to the front entrance. They tended to be tall, well-built young men who never cracked a smile. (Can you blame them?) They stood there all day long. The guns on their hips were visible. Only track personnel like myself with an NYRA badge complete with a picture were let in. In the same scenario as other days, I would get to the workstation around eleven forty-five a.m. and inspect that there weren't any early problems. On this day, there was one. A very petite, good-looking young lady was waiting impatiently outside one of the betting windows. The computers would not open until noon during the week, and she paced back and forth, waiting to bet. The clerk at the window in front of her looked over at me and nodded, telling me he needed a supervisor.

He whispered, "This lady has been trying to place a bet with me for at least ten minutes, and I've tried to explain to her that the betting machines were not activated until noon." I told him I would take care of it, seeing that a bit of sugar usually goes a lot farther than vinegar.

The clerk said that he hoped I could do a better job of explaining things to her. I thought to myself, "What's the big deal?" Within seconds I knew what the problem was. The inside bell went off, meaning it was noon, and the betting machines were open for business. As she tried to walk two or three straightforward steps to the window, I knew the problem. This woman was inebriated. She could hardly walk. Even worse, she could hardly speak in legible words. "I wan a dolly doub," (daily double), and a series of numbers spilled out of her mouth. "Two, two with none, ten with tall."

I politely responded that she wanted a daily double, but what races did she want them for? (On an average day with 9 races, there were 8 daily doubles between races 1 to 8). She pounded on the counter, enraged that we didn't understand her. "If you want the first two races, you can't bet number ten." "Why not?" "Because there isn't a 10-horse in either of the first two races."

At this point, she reached into her skirt pocket and pulled a large wad of money out. As she did, she continued to pound on the window's ledge, screaming profanities at the clerk and me. With the flash of my fingers, I pushed on my walkie-talkie; yes, as I previously mentioned, we used them to communicate back then.

"This is Supervisor Giovanni in the paddock. I have a patron who needs immediate assistance, maybe medical."

Within seconds one of the two Pinkertons came over from the front entrance and asked what the problem was. She started to rattle unrecognizable numbers and names while waving the money in front of his face. As other Pinkertons arrived, they walked her inside the track infirmary, where the doctor on duty gave her some cold water and a warm blanket to sober up. She slept it off, and they escorted her off the track. What she was trying to bet on or for whom we will never know.

Tale 38 -

A Bag Lady Tale

Unlike the last tale, this poor woman could speak perfectly but excuse me, "She looked like something the cat dragged in." It was just a weekday at Saratoga on a hot August afternoon, and I remember there were only nine races that day. This woman approached a window in the upper grandstand to bet a late 8 and 9 race daily double. Her clothes were clean, but I could tell she didn't have much because her ragged dress had holes and tears.

As I walked inside the bay, I made eye contact with her as she approached the betting window. Not trying to stare, I smiled as I walked by ever so slowly. I turned around, passed the last window, and proceeded slowly back through the bay.

What a surprise I had! This woman put an equally ragged purse on the window's ledge and started pulling money out of it like lettuce. I smiled again and watched the clerk count the money she had bet. When finished, he punched her ticket and told her to have a nice day. It was approaching three minutes to post time for the 8th race, and I whispered in the clerk's ear, "What did she bet?"

"A thousand dollar daily double," as he looked down and shook his head in disbelief. "What were the numbers she bet?" I can't say exactly what those numbers were, but let's say 3/4 to keep it simple. I wanted to make a bet, but I had to be discreet. If I wanted to make a bet I had to leave my bay and go out to a SAM (Self Service Machine). It was better not to ask one of my clerks to punch a ticket.

The problem was that it was two minutes to post time, and I still had a few patrons betting. When the last customer left, I went to plan B, the men's room. I opened the stall door and dialed the OTB (Off-Track Betting) number. I choked, trying to get the words out before the horses left the starting gate, but I did! Twenty dollar daily double on whatever the numbers were. Bingo, I got the bet in and hurried back to the TV in the bay to watch the race.

As fate would have it, my horse won the 8th race and paid a big price. If my horse won the 9th race, my double bet would pay out a huge amount. With having a $20 double, my ticket would pay 10 times what a $2 double did. Most of the clerks in the bay sat very quietly as the race was about to go off. This meant word had passed quickly through the bay, and many clerks had bet on it.

Our horse led most of the way, but again it was gambling. We got beat at the wire by the favorite. We had just lost a monster of a bet, and so had the bag lady. You see, this woman was not betting just for herself. She used all small bills, which meant she was betting for many backstretch workers from the horse barns.

We learned the next day that both horses had been hot tips, and these poor people had pooled all their small bills together. This made a single large wager. It was hard to get mad. I lost twenty dollars, but they lost a small fortune.

Tale 39 -

This isn't a Steeplechase Tale

Before 1991, I worked as a mutuel clerk before becoming a Mutuel Supervisor. I was assigned to the paddock area I mentioned in a previous story. This was the green building just outside the main track space where the horses used to be placed in stalls before each race.

Now the paddock is a partially open area close to where the horses and jockeys, et cetera, would meet before every race.

On this particular day, I was pleasantly surprised to see a good teaching friend (whom I rode to work with) stationed at the window beside me. This meant we could talk like we would in the school's faculty room we both taught at. My friend was an excellent handicapper who owned a few trotters at the harness track down the street from the thoroughbred track. We laughed as we counted our start-up money and waited for the twelve-noon bell to ring, officially opening all the betting windows at the track.

My buddy was in deep thought as he analyzed the horses in the first two races to decide whom he would bet on in the first daily double of the day. This was a quiet time; asking questions about betting choices is not considered proper etiquette. Meanwhile, I looked at the Daily Racing Form to decide what I might play.

It was one o'clock, and the buzzer went off, meaning the horses were in the starting gate, and the betting windows were locked. The race went off, and the horses crossed the finish line a few minutes later. I turned to my friend and said, "I'm alive in the double." (I had the winner of the first race).

"So do I," my friend said, but neither of us discussed which horse or horses we had bet in the second race. The buzzer rang again, meaning the first race was official, and the windows were open for betting on the second race. We punched tickets for customers for the next half hour, occasionally making a few wisecracks but never mentioning which horses we had bet in the second half of the double. Around 1:25 pm, the buzzer (bell) went off, signaling that the horses were in the starting gate again and all betting was closed for the race.

We closed our machines down and turned in our seats to face the TV and watch the race. As the horses rounded the last turn toward the finish line at the top of the home stretch, I yelled to my buddy that the horse I bet was ahead a city block and couldn't lose! He looked at me with total disgust because I had just broken the cardinal rule of racing. Never say your horse is so far ahead he can't lose. We turned back toward the TV only to see my horse open up an even more commanding lead. Just then, the curse of what I had said hit. My horse was nearing the finish line and fourteen lengths ahead. Suddenly something spooked him as the horse turned his head to the left and jumped over the fence. My friend was taciturn as he said, "Please don't ever say that again. I bet the same horse as you!" It's called the track curse!

Tale 40 -

A Hoof in the Mouth Tale

I've often spoken without thinking but I wanted to crawl in a hole and die this time. On August 23, 1993, at Saratoga Racetrack, I worked outside the main grandstand and the lower clubhouse. People were lined up all day to get autographs from the Hall of Fame jockey Ron Turcotte. That day, the center of the racing program had a picture of him riding one of the greatest, if not the greatest, thoroughbreds ever, Secretariat.

Ron was sitting outside the clubhouse at a large table dressed in a classy dark suit signing autographs and speaking with the track patrons. He would write whatever you wanted him to and autograph it. He only asked that you make a donation of your choice to the disabled jockey's fund.

I waited until after the 8th race was over when many of the attendees would leave early.

They wanted to avoid the heavy traffic that followed the 9th and last race. My timing was perfect as there weren't any emergency calls I had to tend to. I quietly made my way over to the table as Ron started packing his things up. "Mr. Turcotte, I was one of your greatest fans." "You were, but you're not anymore?" Ron Turcotte was severely injured in a racing accident a few years before and permanently disabled from the waist down. He was in a wheelchair, and when he said that to me, he had a big smile. He was the perfect gentleman. I explained to him that I was the Athletic Director at a nearby school district but worked part-time for NYRA on the weekends during the summer months. He treated me like an old friend and signed a picture of himself riding Secretariat, "To John Giovanni, August 23, 1993," a day that will live in infamy for the rest of my life!

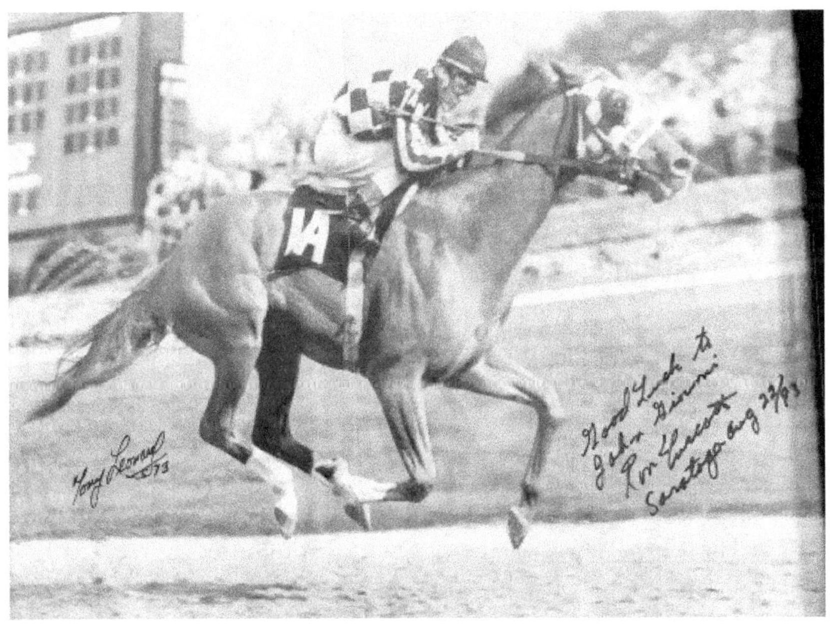

Ron Turcotte aboard Secretariat

Tale 41 -

Another Sister's Tale

Many years after making us late for the first race daily double that sent us home, my sister, Patty Decker (Tale 3), would unknowingly lead to a $723.00 daily double. And to top it off, it was a dollar double, no less, and, with odds exceeding 600 to 1, making it taxable. Don't get me wrong; I'd pay a 20 percent federal tax for a winning ticket like this any day.

The whole scenario began on a day when I decided to reach out to my sister. I intended to wish her a *bon voyage* as she left for a European vacation. She and her boyfriend, John, now deceased, were going on a cycling trip. I was watching live thoroughbred horse racing on cable television when I made a phone call. I called her only to get an answering machine. Obviously, she had already left!

It was midday, and I couldn't remember the track or race. However, looking at the TV, I saw a horse named "Goodbye Pat," or "Pat's Travel." I don't remember the exact name, but it was my sister's name and it had something about travel. The horse was the 12 horse in the race, and from my first novel, "MAC-124," the numbers 124 were my favorite combination. Before this, my wife's New York State License plate was MY 124. Being the big spender I am, I bet a dollar straight, exacta 12-4, and a dollar daily double, 12-4. This is where you have to be very lucky or shitty, as my track friends would say. The 12 horse won the race and paid a massive price to the winner, but the 4 didn't finish second, so I lost my dollar exacta bet. The good news was that I was still alive for a dollar double with the horse in the next race. It won at another high price, and thus my dollar double paid $723.00! My sister had redeemed herself without even knowing it!

Tale 42 -

A Physician's Tie Tale

For many years in Amsterdam, New York, I had one of the most outstanding cardiologists anyone could ever ask for. Not only was he brilliant, but he was also compassionate with a sense of humor. His office staff was equally exceptional. The best part was that he loved horse racing. With Saratoga Thoroughbred track only 25 miles away, he was a true sports fan. I won't disclose his name even though he is retired now and not practicing. However, I will share a witty story.

After a very extensive but good medical check-up, my doctor pronounced me extremely fit to work on the weekends in August as a mutuel clerk supervisor. While still on the examining table, he would talk about horses. We went from the Kentucky Derby to the third race of the Triple Crown, the Belmont Stakes, to the mid-summer derby, the Travers Stakes, at Saratoga. He asked me to sit for a minute as I sat on the examining table to shake his hand (something people wouldn't normally do during COVID-19). "I have to go and get something for you." After a few minutes, he returned with a Macy's Department store box in his hand. It appeared to be a tie box. It was most definitely a tie.

I carefully opened it, and there was a new tie inside. It still had the original store tag on it. It was black, green, silver, and gray with a white background. It had a massive horse with a jockey riding it. It was one of the most hilarious ties I had ever seen, but I accepted it and promised him I would wear it while working at Saratoga.

"I don't like it," he said. "It's yours to keep." I rose from the table, shook his hand, walked to the front desk, paid my bill, took my receipt, and left. It is common in my tales that I don't know the exact day or time, but I do remember seeing the good doctor and his beautiful wife a few weeks later at the Saratoga track. It could have been a Thursday because many physicians in our hometown didn't work on this day of the week.

I was working out in the parking area when I received a call to go to the clubhouse to assist another supervisor with a potential problem. As I started to walk over to the problem area, I turned and walked right into my doctor and his wife. As fate would have it, I had the tie on he gave me a few weeks earlier. I smiled and greeted them, but he had a very unusual grim look on his face. "Are you losing much money?" I jokingly asked him. "No," he replied.

I knew something was wrong but didn't know what it was. I was about to say, "Do you like my tie?" when the Mrs. said, "I bought my husband the same tie."

Reacting somewhat stupidly, I put my foot in my mouth again. "Your husband gave me this tie a few weeks ago at his office. He said he didn't like it."

She looked at him; if looks could kill, he was dead on arrival. She wasn't a happy camper. It might have been the first and only time I've ever seen this woman without a smile. I couldn't excuse myself fast enough as I left the scene of my ineptitude.

Tale 43 -

A Counterfeit Tale

Only once in 27 years of working for NYRA did I encounter counterfeit money passing through our betting windows. It was a hectic day at Saratoga. Approximately 40,000 people were there. Such a large crowd was not unusual for us to have in paid attendance, with lines of people waiting to bet, especially on the weekend.

All of a sudden, one of the clerks started to scream, "John, I've got a big problem!"

I hustled down the bay behind the row of clerks, and this man held up a $20.00 bill to me and proceeded to yell, "This is counterfeit!"

The extent of fake money I had ever seen at the track was a $20.00 bill with a prominent gas symbol on it. Someone gave it to the clerk when it got super busy a little before the betting time was closing. He didn't realize his mistake until he counted his money at the end of the day. The customer received a free $20.00 ticket. The track had the clerk's money and he was out $20.00.

So, when this clerk started to scream, I thought someone had passed a fake bill that anyone could quickly identify. But this was not the case. The clerk handed me the bill and again repeated that it was counterfeit. I put the bill up to a light, and honestly, I couldn't tell at the first examination that it wasn't real. The clerk knew about it because he started to point out what was wrong with the bill. Upon additional inspection, I realized he was right. I instructed him to shut down his window as angry customers waiting in line to bet complained about having to move to another line.

"His machine is broken, I'm sorry for the inconvenience, but you have to move to another window," I politely asked customers. I heard a few profanities uttered as I quickly escorted the clerk to the landline phones in the bay. I called upstairs to the security office, and they asked to speak to the clerk. I could hear them in the background saying someone had just passed $200.00 in counterfeit bills. When the clerk took the phone, he described the criminal as a young man, maybe in his late 20s or early 30s, wearing a blue blazer and gray blue tie. I motioned to him to give me the phone, but it was too late. This wasn't a one-person operation. We had three different people dressed differently, including a woman in a yellow dress. A quick, well-coordinated sting cost the track over $5,000.00. What about the tickets that the clerks had given to these thieves from the counterfeit money? You guessed it. They returned to other windows within minutes of being purchased to cancel them. They got every penny of it. The security investigated, but no one could find a *darn* thing. The trail went dead! These people were not amateurs; they were pros!

Tale 44 -

An Unfriendly Friend Tale

I knew a former colleague whom I considered a dear friend of mine. We never socialized because we were in different classes in high school. We both went to college, got married, and moved on to do our thing. The individual was possibly the most soft-spoken and easygoing person you will ever meet. His wife was exquisite; his children were well-mannered; his family was terrific and classy. I'm sure it would be a friendly meeting if I saw him today. But on this particular day at Saratoga, our meeting was anything but pleasant. I must admit the track was wrong, and he was right in the end! Still, his outburst against me was neither friendly nor ethical.

Not that it made a difference, but I was stationed at the lower grandstand near the top of the stretch that day. There was a problem in another area of the track, and since things were calm at that moment, I decided to answer the call and walked out to the carousel betting windows to help out. No sooner had I locked the bay door behind me and I saw three "friends" from my hometown of Amsterdam, New York. Two out of three friends said nothing and stood stoically next to the third amigo. In an explosive voice, he started yelling that the track cheated him on winning tickets. I tried to calm him down and asked him what had happened. He told me he made a two-horse parlay (A new bet just introduced by NYRA), and both his horses had won, but the payoff wasn't what it should have been. I mistakenly asked if he was sure, and he screamed, "Of course! I'm sure." He wondered what was I going to do about it? I told him the truth. It was a reasonably new bet, and I would get someone to take my call at the carousel and find the answer for him. I asked for fifteen minutes to check out the situation.

Another tirade ensued. He wanted to know why I didn't know the answer now. At this point, I could feel my blood pressure rising, so I quickly turned around to the bay door, unlocked it, and went inside. I made a B-line to the computer room upstairs on the second floor.

Upon arriving, I explained the situation to the technician and added that the bettor was correct. They had not put the proper program into their computer servers.

What does all this mean? Let's say you made a two-dollar bet on a two-race win parlay. Your first horse wins and pays $21.80. Now that amount is a bet on the second half of your parlay. If by chance that horse were to win and pay $20.00 to win, you would collect $218 for your two dollar bet. The computers were not programmed to add the change in, so they would credit you eighty cents, and $20.00 would be parlayed onto the second half of the bet. The total then would have been $210.80. In other words, the bettor would get screwed out of $7.20.

The computer guys said it was an unnoticed glitch and they would have it corrected in a day or two. This didn't help my "old" friend with his bet, and when I returned to tell him the update, he tore me a new rear end. He was entirely right about how the bet should have been computed. However, it still didn't justify his behavior toward me. I apologized for the inconvenience and walked away. That was the last time I ever saw him or talked to him.

Tale 45 -

Count Your Change Tale

You will find dishonest people on both sides of the betting windows at racetracks and other places where gambling is legal. This tale is about how a few people who worked the mutuel windows would make their "tip" money. They did this by not giving the bettors the right amount of change on a winning bet.

How would they do it? It's quite simple. Actually, very simple. However, they understand that their job would be immediately terminated if caught. I had the displeasure of catching two people, and it wasn't a happy departure.

If you have ever been at a racetrack or store and paid with cash, consider how you were given your change. The person giving you your change would hand you paper money first and then your change. The angle here would be to do precisely the opposite. If your total was, let's say, $14.80, the person would hand you the coins first, but instead of eighty cents, three quarters, and a nickel, they would give you three nickels and one dime or twenty-five cents.

Normally, the person puts the coins in their pocket and waits for the bills. They never count the change, only the bills. It doesn't sound like much, but making fifty-five cents or so all day can add to a lot of money. If a patron didn't leave the window and realized they had been short-changed and spoke up, the clerk would apologize. They would ask what they were owed; usually, the bettors weren't sure of the amount. If the bettor returned later and wanted their change, the clerk would again say they were sorry, but it was too late to correct it. Next time at the racetrack, look at the sides of the betting windows. They warn people that the track is no longer responsible for mistakes once they walk away. We received a few complaints from people who said they were short-changed. Each window at the track has a number, so we would start to watch it when more than one complaint came in. The man I caught that day was fired. I told the clerk to shut his window, count his money (I had to watch), and accompanied him upstairs to the mutuel clerk's office.

If they were stupid enough to keep their profit in their money box, they had to record the overage, which stayed with the track. When it was over, my bosses told him he could never apply for any job at NYRA. Someone escorted him off the racetrack. Had he fought, he would have been arrested for theft.

Tale 46 -

A Voucher Mistake Tale

Numerous potential errors were rectified once the IT Staff adjusted the betting machines. Curiously, the more the system improved, the more errors were discovered—a classic case of "the more you know, the more you don't know."

Each bay or betting window at the race track had a single individual stationed at one end exclusively responsible for selling vouchers. While every window at the track was equipped to sell them, it was uncommon for long lines to form at these designated voucher-only spots.

It isn't uncommon for someone to buy a voucher to cover their betting for a few races. Some would go as far as buying one voucher to last them the entire day. The problem was that the clerks had to be very careful because if they hit an extra number, their machine would print a voucher for the wrong amount. That's exactly what this one clerk did. A bettor came to his window and asked for a $100 voucher. You guessed it! He hit an extra zero and gave the guy a $1,000.00 voucher. He didn't realize it until he counted his money between races. This was something the track administration recommended clerks do periodically throughout the day. In this way, they would uncover mistakes and possibly correct them.

This voucher-selling clerk counted his money and yelled for the supervisor's help. I hustled down the bay and asked him what was wrong. "I'm short $900.00." "Count your money again," I commented and added, "Count your money again slowly, and I will count with you."

He counted it again and for a third time. He was still short $900.00. I called the computer room for a printout of his daily transactions. I also instructed the clerk not to open his window after counting his drawer again. He was visibly upset, so I told him to get water, go to the bathroom, or both. Go someplace and relax, but do not return and reopen his window until I instruct you to do so.

I hustled upstairs, and the printout awaited me in the computer room. I started with the last race and worked my way back. It didn't take long to see where a recent voucher had been sold for $1,000.00. Not many people in the grandstand get $1,000.00 vouchers, but maybe someone had purchased this one. Perhaps this $1,000.00 voucher had been used to bet, and money was still left on it. If so, I would freeze it, and no one could bet on it or cash it. Also, if frozen, any winning bets made on it could not be cashed. The IT guys ran the voucher number into the system, and we realized the bettor had seen the mistake ($900.00 over) and had gone to the next bay within minutes and cashed it.

I had the unfortunate job of returning downstairs and showing the clerk his mistake. He gave the patron $1,000.00 by adding one zero to the computer. He argued that he hadn't sold a $1,000 voucher that day, but he did! He was visibly upset, but there wasn't anything more we could do about it. I told him that if he was too upset to work, he could take the rest of the day off but still get his full pay. He refused and went back to work. He said it was good therapy, and he might make some tips.

The IT people quickly responded, trying to prevent that from happening again, but the next day it happened to another clerk. She accidentally gave a patron a $1,000.00 voucher for $100.00. The same thing happened to her. The bettor took the voucher, cashed it, and disappeared. Not the most honest thing to do! The good news, if any, was the IT professionals made a simple change to the system the next day. Any voucher over $100.00 had to be punched not once but a second time before it would print. Fortunately, I never had that problem again.

Tale 47 -

A White Rock Gary Tale

This is another tale about a teaching buddy of mine who had a horse with a big lead coming down to the finish line that jumped over the inside rail fence. That was a second before I said, "We can't lose this race." If you've forgotten, go back to Tale 37, and you will see what happened. If you don't remember, we both lost.

This friend of mine not only worked at the flat track but also got into owning harness horses that ran at Saratoga Harness Track. Incidentally, it was located adjacent to the thoroughbred track we worked at. Whenever one of his horses ran, he would tell the teachers in the faculty room that he thought his horse could win. This man was as honest as the day is long and always said with certainty, "I think we can win tonight."

Back in the early 1970s, Off-Track Betting (OTB) listed their entries not with numbers but with letters in alphabetical order. There was a maximum of eight horses in every race. Thus, you would bet A to H, A being the 1 horse and H being the 8th. I couldn't make it to the track that night, so I went to the local OTB parlor and bet White Rock

Gary (F or 6) with all the horses in the second race. For a two-dollar bet, it cost me $16.00. I was at my father-in-law's house shooting pool with his friends and never found out who had won until later that evening. Another teacher from my building called to give me the good news.

White Rock Gary, the horse I had wheeled (bet with every horse in the second race), won and paid around $32.00 to win. This means that no matter who won the second race, I had $32.00 to win it. There was a big favorite in the second race, and if he had won and paid around $6.00 to win I would have collected $96.00. With a huge payoff, a long shot would win in a perfect scenario. What happened that night was something I had never seen before or ever again at the harness track. I'm sure it has happened, but it is not that often.

The big favorite in the 2nd race lost a wheel on his sulky, and the driver had to pull up his horse and stop. A longshot named "Three Clubs" won and paid over $100.00 to win. My two-dollar F-G double returned around $1,240.00; even though it was taxable, it was and still is the biggest payoff I have ever had. My teaching friend, the horse owner, said he also had hit the double. To my surprise, he said he would have made more money had the missing wheel favorite won. He had a much larger double bet with that horse.

As a footnote, my father's initials were F.G., Felix Giovanni, the winning double letters!

Tale 48 -

A Hundred Dollar Bill Tale

Excuse my repetition; on this given day, I worked at my favorite spot at the track: the outside picnic area. Trees, picnic tables, and television sets provided a beautiful setting to watch the races. I had wanted to bet on a horse that one of the parking lot attendants had mentioned to me. Unfortunately, or fortunately, I got swamped and never got my bet in. The horse I wanted to bet on won, and it paid a decent price. My spirits were deflated, and I was pissed off at myself. As I was aimlessly walking from one set of SAM (Self Service Machines) to another, I smelled hot dogs coming from one of the track vendors in the park. No one said you couldn't eat while on the job, but it wasn't professional. I ran into a few friends who were there eating and drinking while I was working in the same area. One friend offered me a beer, and I gave in. He poured it into a cup, and I remember being in a suit and tie. I still remember the taste of the beer. I thanked him and turned toward the cart path behind me, only to see the Vice President of NYRA on a golf cart with one of my bosses. I dropped the cup and quickly made a path to the side of the concession stand; I wanted to get out of sight! Thank God they didn't see me, but

I saw something while waiting for them to go by. A $100.00 bill was stuck between the canvas and the side frame outside the concession stand. I first thought it was a joke, but I grabbed it anyway. It was a real bill. Where it came from, I don't know and never will. It was amazing how fast my attitude made a huge adjustment in minutes. The hot dog was great, and the big tip made the vendor smile.

Tale 49 -

A Smoking Clerk Tale

During my tenure as a mutuel clerk from 1982 to 1991, I experienced a rare conflict with another clerk. It was unusual since most of the regular clerks were from the New York City area, comprising ninety-nine percent of us, and were genuinely outstanding individuals. Over my twenty-seven years of service at NYRA, spanning Aqueduct, Belmont, and Saratoga, I can confidently say that I encountered only a few individuals who exhibited undesirable behavior.

I don't remember the exact year, but I spent a couple of days working in the lower clubhouse near the finish line during the above mentioned time. The clerk next to me was a regular from Downstate who was a chain smoker. I don't remember if it was even allowed back then, but I believe those who smoked would light up between races as they walked away from their windows. This was why smoking back in the 1980s was overlooked.

What happened took two days of me working next to this clerk. As I mentioned, he was a chain smoker, but to put the icing on the cake, he put the cigarette on his right side, and I was to his right. I was a teacher at that time and had been a High School Varsity Coach. I had and still have a loud voice. If I wasn't sure of a patron's bet, I would raise my voice and ask the person to repeat it to ensure I heard the right thing.

The clerk next to me would take a deep drag on his cigarette as he gazed to his right and stared at me. My blood boiled on the first day I worked beside him, but I shut my mouth. He had another bad habit that could have gotten him fired. If a patron came up to his window and made a large bet, he would lean into his window and quietly tell the person he had a tip on that same horse. This way, he could give out every horse in the race as a tip. People who frequent tracks tend to be superstitious but generous in rewarding the clerk's for a good tip. If they weren't cheap, they would return to the window they bet at and cash the ticket. They figured they had inside information, and as they say, "One hand washes the other."

If one of the many losers returned to his window, this guy would say how sorry he was that the tip had lost. The bettor would vent their anger and walk away. Why? They usually made a much larger bet than planned and were pissed off.

I couldn't hold my temper on the second consecutive day of working next to this guy. I have asthma, and seven to eight hours of breathing smoke had killed me the night before.

The windows opened at noon, and this guy dared to stare at me, cigarette in hand, and tell me I was too loud and he couldn't hear his bettors. Of course not! He whispered his tips so that no one could listen to him beyond a few feet, especially a supervisor who might be walking down the bay behind him.

I exploded! I stood up from my stool and knocked the cigarette out of his hand onto the floor. I stepped on the butt, and in one motion, I grabbed this jerk by the middle of his white button-down shirt. I turned him around and pushed him back against the concrete wall behind us. I screamed that if he ever lit up another cigarette next to me or gave me that stare, I would beat the shit out of him. Excuse my French, but this guy was a real pussy. He never said another word nor lit another cigarette next to me!

Being a regular from downstate, he had a permanent window assignment for the entire Saratoga meet. Since I was part-time, I worked all over the track. We never usually worked at the same window for over a day or two. They would move us around to areas where they anticipated heavier betting traffic.

The tail end of the tale? Not yet. A few years later, I was appointed to a Mutuel Supervisor's position at the track. I was now this guy's boss. As fate would have it, I heard on my walkie-talking that there was a problem in the lower clubhouse. I immediately responded, "Giovanni's got it." I walked into the lower clubhouse, and guess who was at the same window he always had as a full-time employee? Even better, guess who was smoking at his window? I could have had him fired immediately, but like a few years earlier, I didn't. "A look was worth a thousand words." He saw me out of his peripheral vision as I slowly walked behind him and stood there. He tried to be discreet as he dropped his cigarette to the concrete floor and stepped on it. I smiled and slowly walked away from him toward the problem I was called in for. A few of my full-time downstate clerks told me he never smoked at his window again. Mission accomplished!

Tale 50 -

It's Not A Better Than Later Tale

Over the years working at a racetrack, you understand that people who usually are quiet or non-confrontational sometimes become angry and quite volatile over money issues.

It was a scorching early August day, and as the day went on, I got warmer and warmer. Sweat came through my shirt, and my tie and sport coat were stuck to my skin. This tends to make most people fatigued, but it angers a few.

As I slowly walked down my bay behind the column of busy mutuel clerks, I heard someone yelling for my assistance. The clerk had her hands up in the air as if to say, "There's nothing I can do about it." When I reached his clerk's window, I was surprised to see a man from Amsterdam whom I knew by name. He was a few years younger than me, not someone whose company I had ever been in.

I politely asked if there was a problem, not calling him by his name. He exploded like a cannon going off. He wore a sport coat and tie, and his veins popped out of his neck. Once I got him to settle down, he told me that his two daughters had placed a bet at this window, and the clerk had punched the wrong horse numbers.

The clerk said the two girls behind this man had been betting at her window all day. She didn't recall what they had bet because they had made numerous bets that day.

We still had a few minutes to post time, so I calmly told this man I could fix the problem for him. He handed me the two "wrong bets." I asked the clerk to cancel them and give the customer and his daughters their money back or make their new wagers. The clerk gave me a discouraging look as she put each ticket into her machine for cancellation. The screen on the clerk's computer said, "Ticket not a winner," for both tickets. The screen should have said, "canceled," and a dollar amount refund would appear. The clerk handed me the tickets, and suddenly I understood the problem. These wrong bets were from two races ago. There wasn't any way they could get a refund unless they hadn't left the window after they bet. If a clerk makes a mistake and the patron checks their tickets but doesn't leave the window, the error now falls on the shoulders of the clerk. If the race went off and the ladies who made the bets stayed, they would get a refund. It would have been the clerk's error.

In this case, it was two races later. Close to an hour had passed. Nothing anyone, including myself, could do to refund their money. The father of the two girls often came to Saratoga, and he knew he couldn't collect an hour later.

I apologized for the mistake as best I could. He turned to his daughters and called the clerk a few nasty names. It was a poor choice of words that I can't put into this tale.

Tale 51 -

A Betting Trainer's Tale

It is a widely recognized fact that horse trainers take great pride in their achievements, particularly in thoroughbred horse racing. Consequently, when a trainer approaches a betting window and places a substantial wager of four or five hundred dollars on their own horse, it shows a solid chance for their horse to win the race. This practice is entirely legal, and their horse often performs commendable, even if it doesn't emerge as the victor.

Only once in the twenty-seven years of working for NYRA (New York State Racing Association) did I hear of a trainer making a large bet on another horse they had running against them in a race. When it happened, it spread among the clerks like wildfire. Thank God I was overly swamped that day, and the bell had sounded by the time word reached me. This meant the horses were in the starting gate, and all betting was closed for the race.

So, what happened to the hot tip? This trainer had been at more than one window before the race, and word was out around the track. The odds on the horse he was betting on dramatically dropped because everyone was betting with him on the ultimate tip.

What happened next was unique. Did the mystery horse bet down by another trainer win? No! He is still running! But what did happen was that the trainer who made these bets saw the odds on his horse increase drastically and would pay a high price if he won.

What now seems logical is that while the trainer was betting on another horse, he had people from his barn betting all over the track on his horse. The horse he bet on lost, but the horse he trained, won! Might this be illegal? No, but it indeed wasn't very ethical.

Tale 52 -

A Wrong Race Betting Tale

Once again, it's time for another thrilling Belmont Stakes Race, typically held on the first or second Saturday of June (excluding 2021 due to the COVID-19 pandemic). As many passionate racing fans know, the Belmont Stakes is the third and final leg of the esteemed Triple Crown series, with the Kentucky Derby marking the first and the Preakness Stakes as the second.

When a horse manages to secure victories in the Kentucky Derby and the Preakness Stakes, the anticipation surrounding the Belmont Stakes reaches incredible heights. However, I distinctly recall that the Derby and the Preakness were triumphed by different horses, somewhat dampening the excitement. Nevertheless, the Belmont Stakes remains a formidable challenge for these three-year-old competitors, stretching over a grueling distance of 1 ½ miles. It truly takes a robust and resilient horse to emerge victorious in this prestigious event.

I was working in one of the outside betting areas of Belmont Park. I believe it was their old paddock area now equipped with betting windows. We were one race away from the big race, and I heard a yell from around the other side of the bay. "Supervisor, Supervisor," and I rushed to the problem window.

What I encountered was a very unhappy patron screaming at the mutuel clerk. As mentioned in one of the previous tales (50), if the patron has not left the betting window and the race goes off, they can claim a mistaken wrong bet and get their money back. The clerk has to eat it.

I stepped in next to the clerk and asked what the problem was. Also, had the bettor left the window? In a small fit of rage, the patron said he had asked for a forty-two dollar bet on the next race, the Belmont Stakes. The clerk had punched the wrong race, the one that just went off and was now over. As he continued to ramble on about the "stupid" clerk, I looked up at the TV in the bay to see the order of finish for the race that had just finished. I turned back to the patron, who was still creating quite a commotion saying that all he wanted was his forty-two dollars back.

Now, I could play the game, too. The bet he had wanted on the Belmont Stakes had won the race that had just run. He had a winning ticket and didn't know it.

"Sir, you do know the clerk will have to make up the forty-two dollars from his paycheck?" "I don't care," he responded, " I want my money now!"

I responded politely, "Sir, do you realize this part-time clerk is making around eighty dollars in wages today, and you will be taking over half of his paycheck?" "I don't care; I want my money." "Are you sure?" "Yes, I am!" Well, in that case, I will give you your forty-two dollars back. Will that make you happy?"

"Yes, I want my money."

I turned to the clerk and asked him to run the ticket through his machine. He looked at me as if to say it was a loser and would ring up as zero. I nodded to do what I had asked him to do. He did, and to his surprise, the machine screen read Four hundred and some-odd dollars. "So, sir, correct me if I'm wrong. You want your forty-two dollars taken out of the over four hundred winning amount, and the clerk and I can split it?"

The man went silent as I tore into him for being so stupid. As I turned away, I instructed the clerk to pay the man his winnings and that I hoped he had enough class to give him a large tip. I stopped back a few minutes later, and the clerk said he received a fifty-dollar tip and a very apologetic thank you.

Tale 53 -

A Real Rosy Tale

Once again, it was Saratoga, and the year was 2004. I worked as a Mutuel Supervisor stationed in a bay situated in the lower grandstand. However, amidst my duties, I vividly recall the tale that unfolded.

Every bay had one man or woman responsible for the maintenance of the betting machines, and they usually ran every day as situations developed. It could have been a ticket getting stuck in a machine, partially printing, or shutting down. At that time, American Tote Company was the company responsible for all the track betting machines. Thus, the people who worked them were called "totes." If someone had an issue, they would yell, "Tote," and they would be there in a few seconds. If I weren't tied up, I would be right behind them.

I can't recall the specific day or race, but I do remember that the tote was from the south, possibly Kentucky or Maryland. During one of the breaks between races, he motioned me over to the end of the bay, close to the restrooms. In a hushed tone, he told me a secret: "My cousin, Jeremy Rose, is here today to ride a horse in the upcoming race. The horse has been performing exceptionally in training, and my cousin is regarded as one of the finest young jockeys in the entire country."

I told him I'd give him a look and walked into the bathroom for some privacy. I took out my track program and looked at it. I had never heard of the horse, Afleet Alex, or this young jockey. He was 8-10 to one. Just another tip that I will probably lose. I tucked my program into my back pocket and went back to work.

Everyone can figure out what happened next. The horse wins the race and pays a decent price. The tote again approached me and whispered, "Did you bet my cousin's horse?" I just gave him a half smile and said no. End of this tale? Not quite. It's only the beginning.

A few weeks later the same scenario, the tote whispers in my ear, "My cousin's back at Saratoga to ride his horse, Afleet Alex, and he is going to win today." Obviously, the odds were much smaller, so I just passed it off. As good of a horse he might be if he wins, he won't pay diddly. I thanked him and walked away. Afleet Alex won a few races later and didn't pay much, but he did win.

It's Labor Day at Saratoga, the traditional last day of racing. I'm working with my favorite Southern tote again, but his message differed this time. "Mr. Giovanni, my cousin will win the Kentucky Derby in May aboard Afleet Alex."

Eight months later and it's the first Saturday of May 2005. Normally, I would go to New York City and work the race simulcast at Belmont Park. We had a family gathering planned at our house, so I could not work. I went to our local OTB (Off Track Betting) and played Afleet Alex with jockey Jeremy Rose again riding. I boxed him in with 4 or 5 other horses in exactas. (1st and 2nd place). On my way home, I stopped at the supermarket to buy food for our party and ran into my good friend Mike's brother-in-law. His name was Giacomo. There was a long shot in the derby by that name. I had already invested $20.00 on

Afleet Alex, but I drove the four miles back to OTB and put a measly $2.00 to win on Giacomo. Afleet Alex finished third. Giacomo won the race and paid $102.60, my big bet. So, I did win $80.00 on the race, but the horse that came in second, Closing Argument, paid $70.00 for place, and the 10-18 $2.00 exacta paid $9,814.80. The tale gets better or even worse. The two-dollar trifecta, 10-18-12, with Afleet Alex running third, paid $133,134.80. Finally, a dollar Superfecta 10-18-12-17 paid a whopping $864,253.00.

So, I made a few bucks, but you always think your tip horse ran third behind two longshots, and what if you had played the horse that finished second with the two horses you did play? If? As they say in gambling, could've, should've, would've.

Two weeks later, I refused to bet on Afleet Alex in the second leg of the Triple Crown, the Preakness Stakes; Afleet Alex won! Three weeks later and five weeks after the Derby, Afleet Alex won the third leg of the Triple Crown, the Belmont Stakes. Did I bet him? I'm not that smart!

Tale 54 -

Famous People Tales

I've been very fortunate to have met many well-known people at the track, starting with my namesake, Jockey John Giovanni. If you remember, that was in an earlier tale. Many of these people I never met but only smiled and nodded my head as I passed them. Among the people I said hello to was New York Giant's former head coach, Bill Parcells. He would walk through the park to his box seat at the upper clubhouse. I walked by the great actor Larry Hagman in his clubhouse box seat. I said hello, and he started to talk to me. We chatted for a few minutes as I made light of the fact that I lived outside of my hometown Amsterdam in the Village of Hagaman. We had a good laugh, and as his name was just one vowel shy of being the name of my village. I spoke to many NFL Hall of Famers since they had their day at the track every year after the Football Hall of Fame ceremonies in Canton, Ohio. My only regret was that I was a big Paul Hornung fan from his days at Notre Dame and Green Bay, but I didn't dare to approach him. I froze and just stared at him as he studied his program.

Jack Knowlton, the principal owner of the horse, Funny Cide, was very cordial. I asked him if he was enjoying the Belmont Stakes Day, and with a smile on his face, he said, "Yes, but I wish Funny Cide were racing today." (Funny Cide won the Kentucky Derby and Preakness States in 2003 only to lose the third leg of the Triple Crown. The horse that beat him that day was called "Empire Maker." Jack finally had some closure in 2020 as his horse, Tiz the Law, won 'the Belmont.'

Other well-known people I have seen but didn't talk to were Michael Imperioli (Christopher) and now deceased Tony Sirico (Paulie from the Sopranos). Also Judge Jeanine Pirro, while she was running for New York State Attorney General, and the renowned college and professional basketball coach Rick Pitino.

The last person I could think of was a man I couldn't even get close to. I was walking through the box seats at the Saratoga finish line when I received a call to report to the lower clubhouse. All of a sudden, three huge men stepped in front of me. I did my usual smile and showed them my NYRA badge. They asked me to turn around and go the other way. I asked them why. They didn't say a word but stood their ground. I turned around and followed their instructions. Why? Sitting in the clubhouse at the Saratoga Race Course was none other than our Governor, George Pataki, and his family. Later in the day, I walked to a point where I could see them sitting there.

Take 55 -
A Wife's Betting Tale

To this day, my wife, Susan, has never let me forget that she bet the horse named Onion against Secretariat in the 1973 Whitney Stakes at Saratoga. If you remember from Tale 12, my wife won.

Now it's roughly twenty years later, and I'm working as a Mutuel Supervisor at Saratoga. On many days I would take turns driving with a charming man from Amsterdam, Joe Z. I asked him to drive that day because my wife was driving her car to the track so we could go out for drinks and dinner after the races. We had planned to go to the famous trackside bar, Siros, and then head to downtown Saratoga for a romantic night out.

It was the eighth race, and one of my clerks, Mike Danisi, a former jockey, waved for me to come down the bay to his window. Upon arriving, I saw my beautiful wife, Susan, standing before his window. They were talking as she had previously met him through me.

"Your wife wants to bet the ninth race trifecta." Having had a hectic day, I didn't know who was running in the race. I looked up at the odds board and saw what I thought were the 1 and 2 horses as being the favorites. I told her to bet a dollar triple box on 1-2-4 for six dollars. My wife made a bet and said she would see me by the main clubhouse entrance after the race.

Why the number 1-2-4? Besides the fact that the 1-2 horses were the favorites, my wife had a dream many years ago and dreamt those numbers, 1-2-4 triple paying $10,000! A few years later, she received her new car registration and was given the license plate MY-124. (My first novel was MAC-124).

From that time forward, if I liked any of the three horses that were those numbers, I would bet a triple box for $6.00. Just before the race went off, I glanced at the odds board, and the 1 and 2 horses were around 10-1. I thought to myself, what a waste of money. These horses weren't the favorites!

You can guess the rest of the tale. The 1-2-4 combination won, and before it's even official, Susan is at Mike's window, ready to cash her winning ticket. I strolled down the bay toward her, figuring she was anxiously awaiting to do that. She was laughing, as was the clerk, Mike. The race became official, and my wife's ticket, not mine, paid $387.00. Mike counted out one hundred, two hundred, three hundred until he had reached the $387.00. My wife knew what to do. She put $37.00 of her winnings under the window as a tip. The rest of the money entered her purse as she headed downstairs to wait for me. We had a great night in Saratoga Springs.

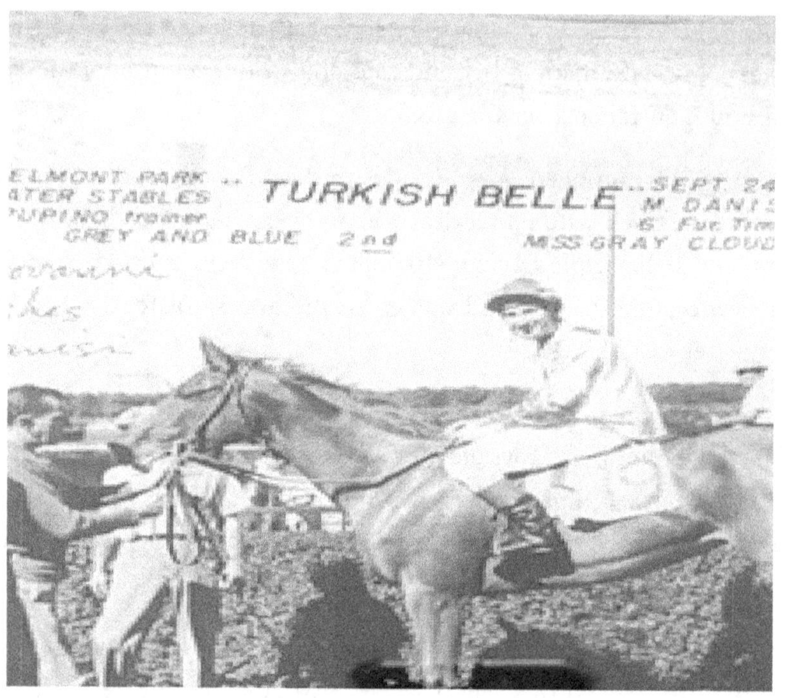

Mike Danisi aboard Turkish Belle

Tale 56 -

A Profanity Tale

I worked at Belmont Park for the Jockey Gold Cup Day of races in late September. I'm unsure of the year, but I believe it was the late 1990s.

Belmont was busy, so the day was going by very fast. Even better, I hadn't had any significant problems after six or seven races. It was a nice relaxing day, but you never know what to expect when it's this quiet. "Shit happens!"

One of the clerks started to waive his hand in the air, so I figured it was a small problem. A situation I could quickly deal with. Upon arriving at the window, I listened to the patron claim he had lost a winning ticket, and he asked if I could help him. I could have if he had another ticket or voucher with the bet he placed before or after it. He did have a losing ticket, and he gave it to me. I explained that I could trace his ticket and try to get his money back. Try, because if someone had found it and cashed it, there wasn't anything I could do.

This is where the patron got a little upset. "What do you mean if no one cashed it? I want my fu*king money now." No reason to express his concern about unlawful carnal knowledge. We all know the four letters that rhyme with duck, and it sure isn't luck.

I explained that I would solve his problem one way or another, but he would have to be patient. Now he started calling me the Duck! He screamed that he wanted to get his money and get out of the track. His profanities drew the attention of a couple of our track officers or Pinkertons. They came over, and he quieted down. I called the computer room and had them run a check on his losing ticket to see if they could find his winning bet.

Now the story gets better! His winning ticket was already cashed, and I knew this guy would not be happy with the news.

By chance, one of my bosses from the upstairs offices, a very mild-mannered man, walked into the bay. He saw the two officers standing next to the patron. I explained what had happened, and that man was about to blow a gasket. My boss and I walked over to the window, and I said that NYRA was very sorry, but his lost ticket had been cashed. With our Pinkertons still on either side of him, he started to scream again, using his favorite "duck" word in every sentence.

My boss interrupted his tirade and asked how much this man had lost on his ticket. I tried to keep a straight face and not laugh - "Two dollars and twenty cents."

I had never heard my boss raise his voice or use profanity. He blew up as he reached into his wallet and grabbed a five-dollar bill. He handed it to the patron and told him to keep the f'ng change. He instructed the officer to please escort this f'ng donkey's ass off the track.

The guy took his five dollars and was escorted off the track. I never heard my boss utter another bit of profanity, but he did have a big smile as he walked away.

Tale 57 -

An Apologetic Triple Crown Tale

The year was 2004, and I was working at the Belmont Stakes again. A horse by the name of Smarty Jones had won the Kentucky Derby and Preakness Stakes. He was now racing for the Triple Crown. The last horse to win all three legs of the crown was Affirmed in 1978, some twenty-six years earlier.

Four minutes before the race was set to go off, the lines of people usually betting until the last few seconds suddenly dispersed. Everyone wanted to get to their seat or any area where they could watch the race.

With everything so quiet, I left my bay and walked up to the concrete walking bridge that overlooked the track on one side. I had a pretty good view of the upcoming race.

The race went off, and at the top of the stretch, Smarty Jones took the lead. I swear the screaming was so thunderous that even the concrete floor below me shook. This crowd of 120,000 fans, the largest live crowd ever to see a sporting event in New York at that time and maybe still today, was going crazy. Everyone, including myself, had waited twenty-six years for a Triple Crown Winner. I had purchased a large racing program and had a $2.00 ticket to win on Smarty Jones. Only $2.00 because I was going to frame it with my program. So, what happened?

Birdstone, ridden by Edgar Prado and trained by Nick Zito, upset Smarty Jones as he beat him to the finish line by one length.

Many people in the crowd started to boo when the horse, jockey, and trainer entered the Winner's Circle. The jockey and trainer were apologizing to the crowd over live televised broadcasts. They felt bad for causing so much disappointment. Winning the Belmont Stakes was an honor and a significant financial return for these men, but they were genuinely sorry for beating the crowd favorite. Both men are class acts!

Tale 58 -

The End of the Tail Tale

I realize that you will always want the best tale for the end. I hope you enjoy the final tail of Tales.

Again, it was the Belmont Stakes, and this tale was an actual doubleheader, I'm not sure of the year, but I think it was 2004 with Smarty Jones racing for the Triple Crown. Ten buses left Albany, New York, full of part-time clerks and ten part-time supervisors like myself—one for each bus. We left around seven a.m. for the approximately 157-mile trip to Belmont Park in Elmont, New York. Little did I know that it would be an extremely long day.

The last race had ended, and people were hustling to their cars, hoping to beat the heavy traffic. I was in charge of one of the bays of betting windows. At the end of each bay, you had one or two windows for people cashing taxable tickets. If your bet pays over 600 to 1, you must go to one of these IRS windows to show who you are and collect your winnings. (A social security card and photo ID had to be presented). I'm not sure what is required today, but you probably still need two forms of identification.

I had only one IRS window in my bay, and as the people left with their winning tickets, they would get in line to cash them. There are a lot of IRS windows at Belmont Park, and usually, there is a line, but within five to ten minutes, everyone is taken care of. It was pushing seven thirty, and most clerks had shut down their windows and were counting their money.

Three or four people were in my IRS line, as this was about the norm unless one customer had a problem and held up the entire process.

A young man, maybe in his mid-thirties, was in line with his wife or girlfriend. He had a winning ticket worth around $1,500.00. The only problem was that he was drunk and refused to show any identification. He said he had lost more than that and wasn't showing an ID or paying taxes. Any ticket that goes into the computer that delivers over the previously mentioned limit cannot be cashed without the identification needed. The transaction can be canceled and returned uncashed to the customer, but the guy didn't want that. He was prepared to stay all night. I stepped back from the window and hit the number 5 on my walkie-talkie for the track Pinkertons. I said I had a problem at my IRS window and gave them the numbers. What I didn't know was that they were so overwhelmed by the record-setting crowd trying to leave the track that unless it was anything more than a major crime being committed, they weren't responding.

It was pushing eight o'clock, and very few windows were still open. As people with winning IRS tickets went by, they saw the open window and got in line. If you have ever been at a mutuel window at a racetrack, you realize bettors get impatient when the line stops moving, and either it is post time, or they want to go home.

The lady with the drunk guy finally heard the grumbling line of people behind them. She conceded to giving the clerk two forms of her identification. The clerk finished the transaction, and patrons got their money minus twenty percent federal withholding taxes. Their ticket paid over $1,000, so the government automatically takes their money off the top. Neither one of them was happy, but they finally left.

It seemed like an eternity, and I knew I would be on the last bus returning to Albany, New York. Usually, everyone would travel in a caravan, so I was probably holding up all ten buses.

A few people in line had given up on the wait and left. They could return on another day to cash their tickets or send them in to be cashed via registered mail.

Now only three or four people were in line, and I expected it to be swift.

That was wishful thinking on my part. The next guy in line had a substantial winning ticket, and you guessed it. I had to withdraw money from a mini dealer to pay this man. He was the person who took your large deposits or withdrawals during the course of the day.

I turned to the dealer and asked him to give the clerk $20,000 to cover this man's winning ticket. As I did, I quickly thought about what would happen if the last few people in line also had big winning tickets. I turned and stuck my face between the metal bars above the window. I asked to see their tickets to determine how much money the clerk should withdraw to pay them. It wasn't much more, but it was enough that I asked the clerk to punch a request for $27,000.

This would cover everyone's winnings. He did, and he turned and handed it to the dealer. Like I've said at least once in my tales, "Shit happens!" The dealer shook his head and said he would have to call downstairs to the money room. He didn't have enough money to cover the payouts.

We were now the last window open at the track. Most track employees had gone home, and now we had to wait for a skeleton crew to deliver the money. They did, but it seemed like an eternity. We paid the people, and I waited for the clerk to count his return money at nearly nine o'clock. As a Mutuel Supervisor, I was the last person to leave the bay.

Upon arriving at the buses, I was surprised that only three of the original buses were there.

When I reached the bus I arrived in, the driver was patiently waiting for me. He informed me that seven buses decided to leave after an hour of waiting. The remaining three would travel together. It was my responsibility to take a head count. I went name by name from my manifest. Forty people were on the bus from Albany, but only thirty-nine were on now. We couldn't leave until the missing person was accounted for. I had his name on my list but not him. I had to walk back into the track and look for my M.I.A. It was to my advantage that the bus happy hour was stocked with everyone's booze, and was almost two hours old! My Manhattans had to wait until I figured it out.

Once inside, one of the mutuel office staff clerks said one clerk had inquired about transportation into New York City. They said they didn't know his name but the description fit. We were leaving with or without him.

Back to the bus, and with a pre-made drink in my hand, we left. End of the trail tale. Not quite! We should have still made it to Albany by midnight. In a perfect scenario, that would have happened.

Our bus driver got stuck at a traffic light, and the other two buses lost us. Our bus driver called the other drivers and told them to keep going. He then assured us he knew the way home.

Two hours into the trip, and now it's Sunday morning. One of the clerks on the bus asked me why we were in Connecticut. He said the sign he saw said Hartford. We were near the capital of the wrong state! Remember, we didn't have cell phones with navigation back then.

I walked to the front of the bus, and the driver said he had taken a wrong turn leaving Long Island and was in the wrong state. Three o'clock Sunday morning, we arrived home twenty-one hours after leaving the previous day!

You know what they say about revenge; it's sweet. Three months later, we again traveled to Belmont Park for the annual Jockey Gold Cup races. Only two buses this time, and I was in charge of one of them. I completed my head count with names before leaving the Albany, New York, parking lot. My missing passenger from June had returned. Before I could ask him about his disappearance, he informed me that he had visited a friend in the city for a few days. To the delight of the entire bus, I ripped this guy a new asshole! Everyone on the bus knew why. A few of them had been on my bus in June.

This is the tail end of my horse tales!

PROLOGUE

Riches to RAGS

By, John Giovanni

Due out in the fall of 2024

Someone once said that the best thing about hitting rock bottom is that there isn't anywhere to go but up! I wish I could believe that.

I move my life's possessions with me everywhere I'm forced to go. They consist of the large cardboard box I carry with me and sleep under, the clothes on my back and a cracked sixteen ounce plastic cup for donations. I stay at any given street corner in Key West until one of the local police officers comes and orders me to vacate. At least it's convenient for me to pick up and move without much fanfare. Actually, the cops down here are pretty cordial. They tend not to bother us until one of the local merchants or tourists complain about us littering up the streets with our foul-smelling and filthy torsos. It costs them more to put us in the jail and give us food and shelter for a few nights.

I had almost lost total sense of time due to the slight changes in the weather. The only way I knew a day had passed was because of the darkness of the nights. I figured I had been out on the streets for around two years. On this day I sat in a doorway with my cardboard house next to me and my plastic cup slightly out on the sidewalk.

"Mommy, can I put some coins into this man's cup?" "No, Courtney, don't go near that dangerous man!" "He doesn't look dangerous, Mommy, can't I just have some pennies to put in his cup? He looks like he needs some new clothes." "Listen to your mother, don't go near him! You never know what diseases he might be carrying!"

"He doesn't look like he's sick, Mommy. I think he just needs a bath and some new clothes." "Courtney, this man is a degenerate who is just playing on the emotions of a five-year-old for sympathy. People like him are useless human beings. They're a disgrace to society, worthless, and should be put out of their misery." "But Mommy, I think if we helped him, he could take a bath and smell better."

Obviously, the smell of urine and fecal matter on my clothes and body were upsetting to the little girl. "Why don't you get a job and work for a living like most of us do," asked the woman. "You could get married and have a family of your own!" "I have a family, Ma'am, they just don't want me," I replied.

With that the irate mother grabbed the little girl's arm and pulled her away from me. As she escorted her down the street, the child twisted around crying and suddenly I saw my own girls crying. Their father had allowed this terrible metamorphosis to take place. It took words from the mouth of a five-year-old to suddenly turbo charge my emotions. This shit was over, now!

I had two strikes against me but there wasn't going to be a third one getting me out. As I had learned many years ago, don't get mad, get even! What I'm about to do will level the playing field of my life and to those who have destroyed it!

www.ingramcontent.com/pod-product-compliance
Lightning Source LLC
Chambersburg PA
CBHW071152130726
47998CB00002B/487

* 9 7 9 8 3 3 0 2 7 2 7 6 1 *